D0000652

When God Was Taken Captive

When God Was Taken Captive

Finding Hope When Heaven Seems Silent

Willard Aldrich

MULTNOMAH

Portland Oregon

Unless otherwise indicated, all Scripture references are from the Holy Bible: New International Version, copyright 1973, 1978, 1984 by the International Bible Society. Used by permission of Zondervan Bible Publishers.

Scripture references marked KJV are from the Holy Bible: Authorised King James Version.

Scripture references marked NASB are from the New American Standard Bible, copyright The Lockman Foundation 1960, 1962, 1963, 1968, 1971, 1972, 1973, 1975, 1977. Used by permission.

Scripture references marked NKJV are from The Bible: The New King James Version, copyright 1984 by Thomas Nelson, Inc.

Cover design by Durand Demlow

WHEN GOD WAS TAKEN CAPTIVE
© 1989 by Multnomah Press
Published by Multnomah Press
Portland, Oregon 97266

Multnomah Press is a ministry of Multnomah School of the Bible, 8435 N.E. Glisan Street, Portland, Oregon 97220

Printed in the United States of America

Library of Congress Cataloging-in-Publication Data

Aldrich, Willard M.
    When God was taken captive / Willard M. Aldrich.
        p. cm.
    ISBN 0-88070-328-8
    1. Hidden God. 2. God—Omnipotence. 3. Providence and government of God. I. Title.
    BT180.H54A43   1990
    231'.4—dc20   89-27543
                                                       CIP
89 90 91 92 93 94 95 96 97 98 - 10 9 8 7 6 5 4 3 2 1

CONTENTS

CONTENTS

INTRODUCTION

How do you write an introduction to a book whose topic seems unthinkable?

That is the problem I face. How can anyone take seriously a book whose title is, *When God Was Taken Captive?*

God is the King of all the earth . . . God reigns over the nations . . . (Psalm 47:7, 8).

I believe this and rejoice in it. How, then, can I believe and ask you to believe that God was taken captive?

And before I try to answer that question, another looms just as large: Even if it's true that God was captured, why should you want to read about it?

Let me answer the second question first.

This book is intended for those who have experienced the inequities of life and have cried out to God to stop the crushing cruelties of man's inhumanities to man. It is one man's answer to the anguished question, "Why?"

The book will bring understanding, healing, and challenge to those who have been bruised and broken when God seems indifferent and absent. It is a book of hope.

It is also a book of comfort. The "absent," "captured" God is present and He is Lord. He responds to the cry of faith. The ark of His presence that was taken captive returned victoriously to Jerusalem. The Lord

Jesus Christ, delivered by God and taken by men to be crucified, is coming again in triumph.

And now to the first question. Why should you believe that God was taken captive? Allow me to give three reasons:

1. The Bible records the fact of it.

2. God caused His own captivity.

3. God's captivity involved only His special, "localized presence" (a term to be defined shortly).

A Captive God?

The captivity of God is first mentioned in the Old Testament story describing the Philistine capture of the ark of God during the days of Samuel. It comes to a climax in the New Testament story of the day Christ was taken captive and nailed to a cross.

In both captivities, God was in control.

The psalmist tells us that in the capture of the ark, God "delivered His strength into captivity, and His glory into the enemy's hand" (Psalm 78:61, KJV). And the apostle Peter tells us that Jesus of Nazareth was handed over to wicked men "by God's set purpose and foreknowledge" (Acts 2:23).

When I say God has been taken captive, do not think I mean that God's throne in heaven has been assaulted and captured. That would not only be impious but nonsensical. But if indeed there is war in the heavens, there is someone who believes it can be done.

This book sees the capture of the ark of God's presence not as an isolated event, but as typical of the way God operates in the world. It maintains that our sovereign Lord significantly limits the use of His divine power and glory. He not only subjects Himself to human governments (which He Himself ordains), but is captive to other self-imposed restraints. And the most paradoxical thing of all is that He uses these very captivities to destroy Satan's world empire and to deliver us from bondage to sin and death.

This book affirms that the Lord God omnipotent rules from His throne in heaven, but that His throne has not yet been established upon the earth. In carrying out His purposes on earth, He sometimes works as a sovereign captive. While He is not visibly, gloriously showing Himself in overwhelming, demonstrable, undoubted power, nevertheless He is surely and faithfully at work in response to the faith of His people.

But captivity in the hands of His enemies—the ark in the temple of Dagon, Christ in the hands of wicked men who crucified Him—is only one aspect of the chains which bind God by His own choosing. God has placed Himself under certain other restraints:

- He is captive to His own character. He cannot act capriciously or out of character.

- He works through a moral plan built on persuasion, not coercion.

- He is captive to sharing sovereignty with His creatures.

- He became captive to the limitations of the incarnation and to indwelling redeemed but sinful human hearts.

- He is bound by His covenants and limited by dependence upon human cooperation.

The seeming absence of God—absent in that He is not visibly, powerfully, and undeniably present and in control—and the plausibility of explaining the universe without Him, set the stage for moral choice. And I believe that God created free moral agents because, more than anything else, He wanted man's free choice of Him under the provisions of grace. Consequently, the temptations of sinners and the trials of trusting saints, where sin is not immediately punished nor virtue rewarded, form the context out of which God saves and transforms those who trust Him.

This book is a call—God's call, I hope—for us to *pray* and to *go* that His kingdom come and His will be done on earth as it is in heaven.

CHAPTER 1

When God Was Taken Captive

I want to tell you the story about the time God was taken captive and to raise the question, "Is it a continued story?"

But first, let me tell you how I came upon the story and began to ponder its significance.

I was scheduled to bring a devotional message for the Guernsey Cattle Association at a vesper service in 1975 at the Thunderbird Inn on the Columbia River north of Portland, Oregon.

Since the Bible makes a number of references to cattle, and since it sometimes compares human behavior to bovine behavior, I thought it would be interesting to show cattlemen how their conduct compared with that of their cows. It appears the cattle often get the blue ribbons. For example:

The ox knows his master, the donkey his owner's manger, but Israel does not know, my people do not understand (Isaiah 1:3).

Samson complained that the Philistines had used his wife to decipher a riddle he proposed to them, saying they had plowed with his heifer (Judges 14:18). Israel was called "a stubborn heifer" (Hosea 4:16). The unequal yoke was forbidden in the words, "Do not plow with an ox and a donkey yoked together" (Deuteronomy 22:10).

In the course of searching the Scriptures for references to cows, I ran across the story of the capture of the ark of the covenant. The Philistines had taken it in battle and subsequently returned it to Israel upon an oxcart pulled by two unbroken and unguided milk cows.

Nothing so amazing in all of this—except that the ark did not seem to be pictured as an empty box. In some sense it contained the very presence of God.

God, somehow, had been taken captive!

So I want to tell you the story about the time God was taken captive—and its possible significance to you and me.

"Don't be silly," you reply. "The idea is unthinkable. Absurd. Who could scale the heights of heaven and assault the throne of God? How could wisdom be outwitted? Omnipotence be overpowered? Omnipresence compressed and put behind bars? Are not the nations as a drop in a bucket before Him?"

Yes, I know. But what power held up for twenty-one days the flight of the angel from God's throne to Daniel (Daniel 10:13)? Who was it who was led captive to a cross?

"But surely you realize that God planned or permitted this," you say. "He was in control. It followed from the determinate counsel and foreknowledge of God."

True, but the captivity was real, and the death real and fearful. Paul adds that Christ was "crucified through weakness" (2 Corinthians 13:4, KJV). God was taken captive, and the blood of God purchased our redemption (Acts 20:28).

But we have gotten ahead of ourselves and have started to read the last chapter when we ought to start at the beginning.

So once upon a time . . .

Evil days had fallen upon Israel. The wicked priesthoods of Hophni and Phinehas, sons of indulgent and weak Eli, were about to end. Their sins were so grievous that God promised He would destroy the household of Eli.

The story unfolds in chapter 4 of 1 Samuel:

> Now the Israelites went out to fight against the Philistines. The Israelites camped at Ebenezer, and the Philistines at Aphek. The Philistines deployed their forces to meet Israel, and as the battle spread, Israel was defeated by the Philistines, who killed about four thousand of them on the battlefield. When the soldiers returned to camp, the elders of Israel asked, "Why did the LORD bring defeat upon us today before the Philistines? Let us bring the ark of the LORD's covenant from Shiloh, so that it may go with us and save us from the hand of our enemies" (1 Samuel 4:1-3).

The earth rang with the shouts of an Israeli pep rally when the ark of the covenant came into the army's camp. But dismay seized the warriors of Philistia. They said,

> A god has come into the camp. We're in trouble! Nothing like this has happened before. Woe to us! Who will deliver us from the hand of these mighty gods? They are the gods who struck the Egyptians with all kinds of plagues in the desert. Be strong, Philistines! Be men, or you will be subject to the Hebrews, as they have been to you. Be men, and fight! (1 Samuel 4:7-9)

What a scenario for God to repeat the miracles of the Exodus! Were not the Philistines ready to acknowledge His power and supremacy?

But they were not quitters, and God had other plans.

How could Israel, ruled by a wicked priesthood and herself ripe for judgment, gain divine blessing by winning a war and escaping judgment? And was not the Philistine perception of the divine presence in the ark ("A god has come into the camp") more perceptive than that of the elders of Israel? Had not the elders reduced God's dwelling place to a fetish? "*It* may . . . save us from the hand of our enemies."

So the Philistines fought. And won!

> . . . The slaughter was very great; Israel lost thirty thousand foot soldiers. The ark of God was captured, and Eli's two sons, Hophni and Phinehas, died (vv. 10, 11).

Seven times in the narrative it is stated that the ark of God was taken captive (1 Samuel 4:11, 17, 19, 21, 22; 5:1, 2). In triumph the Philistines took the ark of God and set it before Dagon, their god. And in a sense, the God whom the heaven of heavens could not contain was captive in the house of Dagon.

Could it be that in that captivity we can find a key to the way He works in our own lives and world?

Should the captivity of God be of comfort and encouragement, or should it bring despair?

Is it possible that this captivity might cast light upon the sufferings and temptations of mankind, even of those who love God and seek to do His will?

And, closer to home, just what does the captivity of God have to do with your problems and mine? If we are "prisoners of hope," bound by sickness, unemployment, divorce, or any of the devastating tragedies of life, how can the workings of the God once captive in Philistia cause our hope to burn more brightly?

Like the disciples who asked, "Can anything good come out of Nazareth?" (John 1:46, NKJV), you may ask, "Can any good come from a God who operates out of prison?"

With Philip I reply, "Come and see."

How Could It Be?

I'm sure some of you are thinking that the whole idea of a "captured" God must be wrong. The very thought is unthinkable!

It does seem quite a stretch of the imagination to make the narrative of a captured ark into a principle of divine operation. A seven-month captivity in Philistia, even a working captivity, is one thing. But to imply, as I have, that this might be a way God characteristically works in a Satan-dominated world—well, that's just too much to accept.

But hold on! It may help to examine the place of the ark in ancient Israel's history and to recognize the actual presence of God in the ark. We will see that God often works in history not from an earthly throne of glory and power, but as the unseen, captive God whose presence and power are seen (only or principally) by the eye of faith.

God's Mobile Home

When the Philistines captured the ark of the Lord, was an empty box all they got? Or was the presence of God dwelling in and about that sacred chest?

To answer that question, we will need to check the biblical account.

In the third month after God delivered Israel from slavery in Egypt, two million Jews came to Mount Sinai where God gave them the Ten Commandments and instructed Moses to oversee the construction of a portable dwelling place for Him (Exodus 19:1-2). God said to Moses:

> Then have them make a sanctuary for me, and I will dwell among them. Make this tabernacle and all its furnishings exactly like the pattern I will show you (Exodus 25:8-9).

The tabernacle, sometimes called the tent of meeting, had two main parts:

1. a courtyard enclosed by curtains;

2. the tent proper, which had two rooms.

A curtain called the veil separated the rooms from each other. The room nearest the courtyard was called the holy place, and in it the officiating priests ate the "bread of God" from the table of shewbread and offered incense and prayers before a golden altar illuminated by a golden lampstand.

God's Living Room

But into the other room, called the holy of holies, the high priest alone could enter. He could do so only once a year, and then only if he carried with him the blood of sacrifice. This was the inner sanctuary, the living room of the house of God. The ark was its only furnishing, variously called the ark of the testimony, the ark of the LORD, and the ark of the covenant.

The ark was a chest made of acacia wood covered with gold. It was approximately three and three quarters feet long; both its height and width were two and one quarter feet.

Four rings of gold were attached to the ark, one at each end of its two longer sides. Poles were inserted into the rings so that the ark could be carried on the shoulders of the Kohathites (Numbers 4:2, 15).

The lid of the ark was covered with gold and overshadowed by two winged cherubim, also made of gold. The cherubim were not idols or images of God, but represented angelic beings charged with portraying and exalting the holiness of God. The lid of the ark was called the mercy seat. God granted forgiveness to his people when the blood of the sin offering was sprinkled on the mercy seat by the high priest on the day of Atonement.

There, at the mercy seat, God promised to meet with Moses and with his people through their appointed leaders and priests. "There, above the cover between the two cherubim that are over the ark of the Testimony, I will meet with you and give you all my commands for the Israelites," God said to Moses (Exodus 25:22).

When the tabernacle was taken down and transported from place to place, God displayed his presence in connection with the ark. So it was when Israel departed from Mount Sinai:

> So they set out from the mountain of the LORD and traveled for three days. The ark of the covenant of the LORD went before them during those three days to find them a place to rest. The cloud of the LORD was over them by day when they set out from the camp.
>
> Whenever the ark set out, Moses said,
>
> "Rise up, O LORD!
> > May your enemies be scattered;
> > may your foes flee before you."
>
> Whenever it came to rest, he said,
>
> "Return, O LORD,
> > to the countless thousands of Israel"
> > (Numbers 10:33-36).

After the death of Moses, the mantle of leadership fell on Joshua. God used him to bring His chosen people across the Jordan River and into the Promised Land. Joshua followed the ark and instructed Israel to do so, saying through his officers,

> When you see the ark of the covenant of the LORD your God, and the priests, who are Levites, carrying it, you are to move out from your positions and follow it. Then you will know which way to go, since you have never

been this way before. But keep a distance of about a thousand yards between you and the ark; do not go near it (Joshua 3:3-4).

On several occasions the ark is equated with the Lord's presence. Such was the case when some Israelites attempted to enter the Promised Land despite Moses' warning not to do so. They disbelieved God's warning that none of that evil generation, except Joshua and Caleb, would enter the land. Moses warned them that "the LORD will not be with you."

Later, to explain their defeat at the hands of the Amalekites and Canaanites, the Scripture states that the ark of the covenant of the LORD did not go with them (Numbers 14:39-45).

When Joshua presented God's strange battle plan for capturing Jericho to Israel's priests and men of war, the LORD's presence is assumed to be in the ark. God directed seven priests to bear seven trumpets of rams' horns before the ark of the LORD in procession around the city. When the instructions were carried out, the priests and the rams' horns are described simply as being before the LORD. The clear implication is that God was present in and with the ark (Joshua 6:4, 8, 11, 13).

One of the darkest stories of human degradation found in the Bible is the account of the rape and murder of a concubine at the hands of the men of Gibeah. These men were from the tribe of Benjamin, and their kinsmen defended rather than condemned them. In response, all Israel gathered against the Benjamites to punish their depravity. But Israel's own spiritual condition must have been suspect, for God allowed the Benjamites two days of victory in which they slaughtered thousands of their brothers.

And the Israelites inquired of the LORD. (In those days the ark of the covenant of God was there, with Phinehas son of Eleazar, the son of

Aaron, ministering before it.) They asked, "Shall we go up again to battle with Benjamin our brother, or not?" The LORD responded, "Go, for tomorrow I will give them into your hands" (Judges 20:27-28).

In this crisis, God answered from the ark. He met with His people and spoke to them from above the mercy seat between the cherubim, just as He promised Moses He would do.

What Does It Matter?

All this should make it clear that the ark was indeed the special dwelling place of God among His people. It was the heart of the sanctuary in which they approached Him to worship. It was His communication center from which He spoke with them. It was His field headquarters and His chariot when He led His chosen people into battle (1 Chronicles 28:18).

Consequently, when 1 Samuel repeats seven times that the Philistines took or captured the ark, we have reason to believe that the localized, operational presence of God was in and with the ark.

But how can this be? Does not the psalmist declare God to be present everywhere?

Where can I go from your Spirit?
    Where can I flee from your presence?
If I go up to the heavens, you are there;
    if I make my bed in the depths, you are there.
If I rise on the wings of the dawn,
    if I settle on the far side of the sea,
even there your hand will guide me,
    your right hand will hold me fast.
If I say, "Surely the darkness will hide me
    and the light become night around me,"
even the darkness will not be dark to you;
    the night will shine like the day,
    for darkness is as light to you (Psalm 139:7-12).

It seems as though the psalmist's confidence that God is present everywhere is built upon the idea of multiplied local presences: in the heavens, in the depths, on the wings of the dawn, and on the far side of the sea. Other Scriptures tell of God's special presence in a variety of circumstances:

Adam and Eve fled from His presence in the Garden of Eden.

Abraham met Him on the plains of Mamre.

Jacob dreamed of the ladder reaching from earth to heaven and awoke to say, "Surely the LORD is in this place."

Moses stood before Him at the burning bush.

Jonah fled from the presence of God.

Jesus said, "Anyone who has seen me has seen the Father" (John 14:9). And again, "It is expedient for you that I go away: for if I go not away, the Comforter will not come unto you" (John 16:7, KJV).

The time-and-place localized presence of God may be in heaven or on the earth. On earth it may take the form of holy wrath in "the Spirit of judgment and burning" as Isaiah described it—like a magnifying glass focusing the sun's rays into a burning power. His localized presence may be like that of an outpost in a mission station in Satan's territory.

God's presence may also be an unseen but real presence as His Spirit bears witness with our spirit. The psalmist talked about it in terms of the shepherd's rod and staff which brought comfort and dispelled fear (Psalm 23). It is also a conditional presence as found in the promise, "You will seek me and find me when you seek me with all your heart" (Jeremiah 29:13).

God's Presence like the American Presence

Perhaps we can think of God's presence as something like the American presence around the world. Embassies, consulates, warships, armies, tourists, Singer sewing machines, and Coca Cola all represent America.

No foreign power has ever defeated and conquered mainland America, yet American embassies have been bombed, peacekeeping forces have been killed or driven out, American planes have been hijacked, and American citizens taken hostage. In many parts of the world, the American presence is hated and harassed.

In a similar way, God's presence on earth is hated and hunted by Satanic forces. God's localized, operational presence often seems captive to the world government of the evil one, yet no power has assaulted the gates of heaven and taken God's homeland captive. In His very "captivity," God works powerfully to accomplish His purposes. He is a God of a million experiences at once.

Captured, Not Impotent

In a passage we shall examine more closely in the next chapter, the psalmist says God "delivered His strength into captivity, and His glory into the enemy's hand" when the ark was captured (Psalm 78:61, KJV).

If you are offended by the idea that *God* was taken captive, please remember that *God* sent the ark of His strength into captivity. Perhaps you are unconvinced that the capture of the ark is a good way to picture God's operation in the world; but will you at least entertain with me the idea that God has placed several limitations upon the use of His strength and glories, and that these could well be called self-imposed captivities?

I hope that in the following chapters you will come to see that the Lord God omnipotent, whose throne is established forever in heaven, has yet to establish His throne upon the earth—and, amazingly, that the Lord of might and glory has allowed Himself to be taken captive.

But before then, let us joyously proclaim with the psalmist,

> The LORD is in his holy temple;
>> the LORD is on his heavenly
>> throne (Psalm 11:4).

And as instructed by our Savior, let us pray,

> Your kingdom come,
> your will be done
>> on earth as it is in heaven (Matthew 6:10).

Let us add also this prayer concerning the future, earthly enthronement of the true King:

> Lift up your heads, O you gates;
>> be lifted up, you ancient doors,
>> that the King of glory may come in.
> Who is this King of glory?
>> The LORD strong and mighty,
>> the LORD mighty in battle.
> Lift up your heads, O you gates;
>> lift them up, you ancient doors,
>> that the King of glory may come in.
> Who is this King of glory?
>> The LORD Almighty—
>> he is the King of glory (Psalm 24:7-10).

CHAPTER 2

The Binding of Omnipotence

CAN God really be bound?

Can the Creator of the universe, the One who set the stars in place and sent the planets into orbit, be confined?

The idea sounds preposterous, unthinkable, absurd. And yet . . . The very Bible that tells us of God's limitless power and sovereignty also records that Israel's enemies, the Philistines, captured the ark of God and carried His "strength and glory" into their camp and into the house of their god.

That same Bible declares that at the crossroads of prophecy and history, the chief priests, elders, and the whole council of Israel "bound Jesus, and carried him away, and delivered him to Pilate" and to death (Mark 15:1, KJV). This Jesus was the One in whom dwelt all the fullness of the Godhead bodily (Colossians 2:9, KJV). To Him had been given all power in heaven and on earth. Twelve legions of angels were at His beck and call.

And yet He was bound and delivered over to be crucified.

That isn't the whole story, of course. We know that even while Christ was bound and delivered over to crucifixion "through weakness" (2 Corinthians 13:4, KJV), He bound and plundered the powerful Evil One and set his captives free (Colossians 2:15; Hebrews 2:14-15).

Which raises a question: If Christ bound the Strong Man of evil, entered his house, and plundered his goods, who then can bind Omnipotence, enter His house, and plunder His goods? Certainly, neither angel nor man can do it, unless for some reason God permits it. *If God Almighty is in any way bound or taken captive, it must be a binding He Himself chooses.* It is absurd to think otherwise.

James DeLoach, associate pastor of the Second Baptist Church of Houston, expresses something of this truth in a devotional article titled "God Ain't Dead."

> I am not a connoisseur of great art, but from time to time a painting or picture will really speak a clear, strong message to me. Some time ago I saw a picture of an old burned-out mountain shack. All that remained was the chimney . . . the charred debris of what had been that family's sole possession. In front of this destroyed home stood an old grandfather-looking man dressed only in his underclothes with a small boy clutching a pair of patched overalls. It was evident that the child was crying. Beneath the picture were the words which the artist felt the old man was speaking to the boy. They were simple words, yet they presented a profound theology and philosophy of life. Those words were, "Hush child, God ain't dead!"
>
> During recent years, some members of our church have suffered crippling financial losses,

break-downs in their bodies, and crumbling families. What can we say to these dear friends? What kind of hope do they have? What kind of hope do we have?

That vivid picture of that burned-out mountain shack, that old man, the weeping child, and those words "God ain't dead" keep returning to my mind. Instead of it being a reminder of the despair of life, it has come to be a reminder of hope! I need reminders that there is hope in this world. In the midst of all of life's troubles and failures, I need mental pictures to remind me that all is not lost as long as God is alive and in control of His world.

Yes, God is in control, and this is true *even when to all appearances the very opposite seems true*—even when, for example, Communist guerrillas are gunning down Christian missionaries.

God's Presence in Enemy Territory

The psalmist Asaph makes it crystal clear that God limited Himself at the time the ark was taken captive by the Philistines. In Psalm 78 he recounts the faithfulness of God in delivering His people from bondage in Egypt, in caring for them in the wilderness, and in bringing them into the Promised Land. Yet at the same time Asaph reminds Israel of her repeated periods of unbelief and rebellion. These reached a climax in the time of the judges, provoking God to anger against His people. Here is how he puts it:

> They angered him with their high places;
>> they aroused his jealousy with their idols.
> When God heard them, he was very angry;
>> he rejected Israel completely.
> He abandoned the tabernacle of Shiloh,
>> the tent he had set up among men.

> He sent the ark of his might into captivity,
> > his splendor into the hands of the enemy.
> He gave his people over to the sword;
> > he was very angry with his inheritance
> > (Psalm 78:58-62).

God Sent His Power and Glory into Captivity

"*He* sent the ark of his might into captivity," the New International Version text says. The Philistines did not overpower God, nor did they catch Him at a weak or sleepy moment. God *sent* the ark of His glory into the hands of the enemy.

That statement is surprising enough, but the Hebrew text seems to go even further. The original makes no reference to the ark at all. The word is supplied by the translators to help us better understand the historical background of the psalm. Could it be that the original's lack of reference to the ark emphasizes that God "delivered *his strength* into captivity, and *his glory* into the enemy's hand"? The translators of the King James Version thought so, and rendered it in that way.

The ark was the focal point of God's presence in the tabernacle and temple. From above the mercy seat and through the high priest, God communed with His people. The ark was therefore not only the symbol, but the unique and special place of God's presence among His people.

Because God's people spurned His love and defied His commands He "abandoned the tabernacle of Shiloh" (Psalm 78:60). But when God sent the ark of His might into captivity, did He send it empty into the hands of the enemy?

No. Clearly no. He "delivered his strength into captivity, and his glory into the enemy's hands."

To represent God's power and glory as bound and somehow limited while God Himself rules from His throne in heaven is completely consistent with our common use of the word "captivity." It may refer to simply a part of us. We say, "Something captures my imagination," and we are encouraged to "bring every thought captive" to Jesus Christ. Or again, our bodies may be captive even while our spirits are free.

The paradoxical triumph of the captive power and glory of God is seen in the sacrificial death of our Lord Jesus Christ as pictured in Hebrews 1:3 (KJV). Note the reference to His glory and power, delivered captive unto death to purge our sins, and His ultimate triumph. This is God's Son, "who, being the brightness of his *glory* and the express image of his person, and upholding all things by the word of his *power*, when he had by himself purged our sins, sat down at the right hand of the Majesty on high."

Please remember that when we talk about "binding omnipotence" or "taking God captive," we must be clear that this is a self-imposed limitation. God *permits* evil to exist; He is not powerless because of it.

Nor is He incapacitated by it. He is not like Adoni-Bezek, a Canaanite king who was captured by the tribes of Judah and Simeon and was rendered helpless after they destroyed his vast army. They cut off his thumbs and big toes and thus made him unfit for battle. It seems that this was a nasty but common practice of the day. Adoni-Bezek had engaged in it, according to his own word: "Seventy kings with their thumbs and their big toes cut off have picked up scraps under my table. Now God has paid me back for what I did to them" (Judges 1:7).

Further, we must remember that the world is, after all, a mere speck in the immensity of God's vast creation. And Satan's power and man's day of defiance against God are as a vanishing vapor in comparison to the unending days of eternity.

What Is Self-Limitation?

The captivity of Judah and the looting of the temple by Nebuchadnezzar show how God sometimes achieves

His purpose by choosing not to exercise His power for the protection of His people. The most high God who rules in the kingdoms of men (Daniel 4:17) delivered Jehoiakim king of Judah—along with sacred articles from the temple—into the hands of the Babylonians. Nebuchadnezzar took these treasures from Jerusalem and put them into the house of his own god.

What a seeming defeat for the LORD, the God of Israel, that His very temple treasures would fall into the hands of Nebuchadnezzar! And yet it was He who saw to it that they were kept and returned when the captivity ended seventy years later. Five thousand four hundred articles of gold and silver were thus preserved and returned to their place. Even the temple itself was rebuilt by the order of Cyrus, king of Persia, whose heart was stirred by the LORD God of heaven (Ezra 1:1-11).

God Is Captive to His Own Character

Speaking of God's "captivity" or "self-limitation" naturally brings up questions regarding His character, His attributes. If God is both sovereign and all-powerful, does His might make right? Or does right limit might? Is God above moral restraint? Is He beyond the demands of justice and fairness?

One bedrock conviction stands at the forefront of this discussion: God is the source and standard of what is right. Nothing outside or above Him determines what He should be or how He should act.

Nevertheless, God is not capricious or arbitrary. Being light and love, can His ways be darkness and hatred?

Sometimes men portray God's sovereignty as fickle and absolute like that of a tyrannical king who dominates and bullies his subjects without regard to law or justice. But God cannot be like that. Abraham expressed as much when he asked, "Will not the Judge of all the earth do right?" (Genesis 18:25).

Something planted deep within us insists that there is such a thing as right, and that God is righteous and just in all His ways.

John Calvin, the great reformer, is sometimes accused of exalting the sovereignty of God above His moral attributes, thus freeing Him from all restraints. But Calvin sought to safeguard himself from attributing pure caprice to the will of God. A. Mitchell Hunter says that Calvin taught, "God does not display caprice but exercises freedom limited only by the restraints of His own nature. . . . There are necessities of His nature which constitute law to Him. . . . It is not less necessary for Him to be good than to be God."[1]

He Is Faithful to Himself

So God is captive to His own character; He is faithful to Himself. In the words of Paul, "He cannot deny himself" (2 Timothy 2:13, KJV). He rewards those who by faith diligently seek Him and He promises that those who suffer with Him shall reign with Him—but that He will deny those who deny Him (Hebrews 11:6, 2 Timothy 2:12, KJV).

Certainly God can do everything He wants to do, but He does not want to do everything He conceivably could do. He will not violate His holiness, wisdom, and love. He cannot act capriciously. Everything He does conforms to His holiness.

To say that God is captive to His holiness might better be expressed by saying He is unchangeable in holiness. What He does must conform to His holiness.

This includes the forgiveness of our sins. Yes, forgiveness is captive to God's holiness.

How, then, can He be free to forgive sins?

I'm glad you asked. My answer may sound like a page out of a theology, but wade through it with me. It's important! It's more than man-made theology. It is the heart of the Christian faith.

God's Forgiveness Bound by His Holiness

Because God is holy, He cannot condone sin nor forgive it in violation of His holiness. God expresses His holiness in s*tatute* laws and *natural* laws, both of which reward righteousness and punish evil. Both God's commandments and His providences teach that "the wages of sin is death" (Romans 6:23) and "the soul that sinneth, it shall die" (Ezekiel 18:20, KJV). Sin always leads to death, for it alienates the sinner from the Author of Life. Sin cannot merely be ignored. Sin is *real,* it is an offense to God, and overlooking it will not make it go away. It must be dealt with. That is why Christ had to die in our place; He satisfied the demands of God's holiness on our behalf. In the words of the apostle Paul, "Christ died for our sins according to the Scriptures" (1 Corinthians 15:3).

Let me illustrate.

I once was privileged to present the Christian understanding of the Mosaic sacrificial system at a meeting between rabbis and evangelical Christians. It was my hope that my Jewish friends might see that the death of Christ was according to Scripture and was a fulfillment of the animal sacrifices prescribed in the Hebrew Scriptures.

The law, I said, required that a sacrificial animal be slain and its blood be shed in order to "cover" (or "atone for") the sins of the worshiper: "It is the blood that makes atonement for the soul" (Leviticus 17:11, NKJV). "Without the shedding of blood there is no forgiveness" (Hebrews 9:22). Having in mind that the blood of goats and bulls could not "take away" sin—that is, pay its deserved penalty so that God would be satisfied—but that Jesus Christ, as the Lamb of God, did take away the sin of the world, I asked, "Wouldn't it be wonderful to think that God Himself fulfilled the sacrificial system?"

Three rabbis simultaneously declared that there was nothing in the sacrificial system requiring a better sacrifice. Nothing in the nature of God, they said, demanded that His holiness be satisfied and His righteous government be upheld before He could forgive sin.

But is this true? What of Israel's history, replete with examples of God's wrath being poured out on a sinful and unrepentant nation offensive to His holiness?

God's holy indignation is like a hurricane which runs its destructive course, spends its fury, and comes to rest. Thus Ezekiel foretold the destruction of rebellious Jerusalem and its inhabitants when God sent Israel into captivity in Babylon:

> "So as I live," declares the Lord GOD, "surely, because you have defiled My sanctuary with all your detestable idols and with all your abominations, therefore I will also withdraw, and My eye shall have no pity and I will not spare.
>
> "One third of you will die by plague or be consumed by famine among you, one third will fall by the sword around you, and one third I will scatter to every wind, and I will unsheathe a sword behind them.
>
> "Thus My anger will be spent, and I will satisfy My wrath on them, and I shall be appeased; then they will know that I, the LORD, have spoken in My zeal when I have spent My wrath upon them" (Ezekiel 5:11-13, NASB).

God's righteous wrath is satisfied when it is spent upon the wicked who deserve it, and His holiness is appeased or "comforted."

But in the New Testament we learn that God, in His great love and mercy, provided a Substitute for guilty sinners, One who willingly took our place and endured the wrath of God that we deserved.

It helps us to understand the death of Christ as a sacrifice for our sins when we see it in the light of Ezekiel

5:13, but with this difference: In Ezekiel God's wrath is spent upon the guilty who deserve it. In the death of Christ as our substitute, God's wrath against sin was fully poured out against His innocent Son, our Savior. Only in this way could God's holiness be satisfied. This satisfaction of God's holiness is called *propitiation* in Romans 3:25 (KJV).

In that passage the apostle revealed that God's longing to forgive us hinged on—or was captive to—His own holiness and righteousness. Paul wrote that God set forth Christ Jesus to be a propitiation through faith in His blood to declare His righteousness for the forgiveness of sins that He might be just and the justifier of him who believes in Jesus (Romans 3:25-26, KJV). When God's holiness was satisfied and righteousness was declared, God was set free to forgive sin.

The morning reading in *Daily Light* for May 6, 1988, contained a compilation of Scripture verses concerning divine justice and mercy which greatly comforted my wife and me the day we took a loved one into court for the crime of theft.

He was being judged under a "diversionary program"—a probationary route as an alternative to a prison sentence. I was practically overcome as I read:

Mercy and peace are met together; righteousness and peace have kissed each other.

A just God and a Savior.

The LORD is well pleased for his righteousness' sake; he will magnify the law and make it honorable.

God was in Christ, reconciling the world unto himself, not imputing their trespasses unto them.

These and the verses which followed beautifully expressed God's provision for forgiveness, and seemed to exactly match our need as we prepared to enter the courtroom.

God Is Bound by His Love

God is captive to His love as well as to His holiness. If "the love of Christ constrains us" (2 Corinthians 5:14, NKJV), how much more must the Source of that love be constrained to reach out in saving grace to a lost world? Love being what it is, how could God, who is love, have done otherwise? How precious to think of God "held in custody" by His love to come to our rescue! How terrible to imagine Him otherwise! As the apostle Paul was "bound in spirit" to visit Jerusalem in spite of threats to his safety, so was Jesus bound in spirit, captive to His sacrificial love for lost humankind.

Anna Dubinetzki well knows the compelling force of love. Twice it saved her life; once it drove her halfway around the world.

Her story began almost fifty years ago as German SS troops ruthlessly crushed the Warsaw Ghetto uprising. Anna's Jewish parents—knowing their days were numbered—lowered their beloved daughter over the ghetto wall in the desperate hope she would be found and cared for by outsiders. "The child's name is Anna and her birthdate is October 13, 1942," said a note hastily scribbled by her parents. "May God protect her and you who have found her."

On May 15, 1943, Alvin Dubinetzki was on his way to work when he spied a moving bundle of rags lying along the Warsaw ghetto wall. The tall, former lieutenant-colonel in the Polish army scooped up the bundle, looked inside, and hurried home. He called for his wife, Stefanja, and the couple, moved by love, decided to adopt the pretty little girl—fully aware that her Jewish ancestry would mean their execution should they be discovered by the Nazis. Disregarding the danger, the Dubinetzkis embraced Anna and reared her as their own.

The whole story came to light in April 1989 when Anna traveled to the Yad Vashem (Holocaust) Memorial in Jerusalem to receive, on behalf of her now-deceased adoptive parents, the "Religious Gentile" award. Love prompted her to make the journey to Israel, just as it is love that moves her to seek the identity of her true parents.[2]

It was also love compelled to sacrificial action that prompted two men to brave the icy waters of the Potomac several winters ago. A departing commercial airliner had clipped a bridge and crashed, spilling passengers into the freezing river. One onlooker spotted a drowning passenger, dove into the freezing waters, and towed the passenger to safety. Another man twice refused a life preserver, choosing instead to hand it to someone else. When at last a third preserver was thrown his way, he had disappeared—sucked beneath the icy waters to his death.

Jesus said, "Greater love has no one than this, that he lay down his life for his friends" (John 15:13). But these were strangers, saved by men captive to love.

God Became Captive to Incarnation

God's love for mankind prompted Him to send His Son into the world to become our Savior. "In this the love of God was manifested toward us, that God has sent His only begotten Son into the world, that we might live through Him" (1 John 4:9, NKJV).

His coming was not that of an extraterrestrial making a state visit via UFO. Rather, He became one of us by being born into the human family through the virgin birth—a union of God and man. We call it the Incarnation—the Word becoming flesh (John 1:14).

The Incarnation became the ultimate self-limitation or captivity of God. He sent His strength into captivity, His glory into the hands of the enemy.

The apostle Paul tells us that Christ emptied Himself, giving up the form of God and taking the form of a servant. And then He humbled Himself and became obedient unto death, even the death of the cross.

The apostle John tells us that the world failed to recognize Him or to welcome Him. God's incarnate power and glory were captive in enemy territory, yet revealed to some, who could say with John, "we beheld His glory" (John 1:14, KJV).

The manner in which Jesus lived and finished the work God gave Him to do instructs those of us who also live and work in a Satan-dominated world.

Shortly after the birth of Jesus, an angel warned Joseph to take the infant into Egypt in order to save Him from death at the hand of Herod (Matthew 2:13).

Joseph brought Jesus back to Israel following the death of Herod (Matthew 2:19), but not to Judea, because Archelaus, Herod's son, was ruling there. Instead, the holy family fled into Galilee.

The public ministry of Jesus was characterized by strategic withdrawals from one region to another to escape the opposition of the rulers. He left Nazareth and went to Capernaum in Galilee following the imprisonment of John the Baptist (Matthew 4:12). Upon learning of John's death He departed across the sea of Galilee by boat alone (Matthew 14:13). The Pharisees took counsel against Jesus to destroy Him after He healed a man with a withered hand on a Sabbath. "But when Jesus knew it, He withdrew from there . . ." (Matthew 12:15, NKJV; see also Mark 3:7).

After strenuous preaching and healing campaigns, He withdrew into the wilderness for prayer (Luke 5:16). He withdrew from the five thousand whom He had fed with loaves and fishes because they sought to take Him and make Him their king (John 6:15).

We cannot fathom the extent of the mental captivity which took place when Christ emptied Himself so as to join a human nature and to develop as a child who grew in wisdom and stature and in favor with God and man (Luke 2:52). Was there a time when He had less wisdom?

And the King of kings and Lord of lords paid taxes to a hostile government.

And finally, He submitted to arrest, humiliation, and crucifixion. But even there He was in control and set the date of His execution for the day of the Passover—in spite of the counsels of the chief priests, the scribes, and the elders (Matthew 26:3-5).

God Is Bound by His Covenants

From the very beginning, God made promises to mankind which He obliged Himself to keep. These promises often came in the form of *covenants*. The Lord has bound Himself to them; He will not violate them.

That God is captive to His covenants should greatly encourage us. God confirmed His promise to bless Abraham by taking an oath (Hebrews 6:13, 17). And when we believe God and focus our faith upon Abraham's Seed, the Lord Jesus Christ, our faith is "counted for righteousness," and we are made heirs of the promise of the Holy Spirit (Romans 4:3-5, 16; Galatians 3:13-14). God has bound Himself to keep this covenant of salvation. He is captive to it.

Early in the history of Israel's deliverance from slavery in Egypt and entrance into the Promised Land, God threatened to destroy the rebellious nation and to begin again with Moses and his descendants. But on the basis of the covenant made with Abraham, Moses pled with God not to blot out the nation. And, captive to His covenant, "The LORD relented and did not bring on his people the disaster he had threatened" (Exodus 32:14).

We have the assurance that as long as the earth lasts and the stars remain in the heavens, God will be faithful to His covenant of salvation (Jeremiah 31:35-36, 33:20-26, Hebrews 10:16-17). He is bound to it by His own holy name.

God Is Bound by His Plan

God is not only captive to His own character and covenants, He is captive to His eternal plan. It sounds odd to speak of God being bound to a plan He Himself freely devised, but it's true nevertheless. Captivity comes to mean God's sovereign commitment to self-limitation of His power and prerogatives.

God Himself sets the example for the man "who keeps his oath even when it hurts" (Psalm 15:4). His word is as good as His bond. God is bound by His character, His covenants, and His plan.

On a smaller scale, I experienced something like this recently. I was on my way to conduct a funeral and decided to give the honorarium to a married student at Multnomah School of the Bible. On the way home from the funeral I opened the envelope handed to me by the funeral director. In it was a note from my deceased friend to his wife, requesting that I conduct the service and be paid not less than two hundred dollars. The envelope contained two one-hundred dollar bills and one fifty.

When I vowed to give away the honorarium, I was thinking in terms of fifty dollars at the most. Could I fulfill my vow and give only the fifty? No, the entire two hundred and fifty dollars must go to my friend. And it did.

In a similar way, God is captive to His character and His covenant promises.

Here is what the Lord Himself had to say: "The LORD Almighty has sworn, 'Surely, as I have planned, so will it be, and as I have purposed, so it will stand'" (Isaiah 14:24). Indeed, He ". . . works out everything in conformity with the purpose of His will" (Ephesians 1:11).

In what ways has God bound Himself to His plan? We will look into that extraordinary question next.

Chapter 2, Notes

1. A. Mitchell Hunter, *The Teaching of Calvin*, 2d rev. ed. (Old Tappan, N.J. : Fleming H. Revell, 1950), p. 56.

2. *The Jerusalem Post*, 11 March 1989.

CHAPTER 3

Would You Do Things Differently?

HAVE you ever thought that if you were God, you would do a lot of things differently? You would replace drought with abundance of rain, change bitter cold to California sun, banish tornadoes, prevent earthquakes, flatten tidal waves, stifle volcanoes. And, especially, you'd keep brutal men from terrorizing the innocent.

It is hard to understand, in the face of extreme human depravity, why God does not break His silence, and immediately and unmistakably strike down the wicked. Why does He restrain His anger? Why does He allow the very atrocities He says He hates? Jesus said it would be better for child-abusers to hang millstones around their necks and to be thrown into the sea than to continue in their evil.

Where are the millstones? And where is God?

Almost fifty years ago Elie Wiesel was a fifteen-year-old prisoner in the Nazi death camp at Buna. He recalls the horror of the camps more vividly by one scene than by citing all the camp statistics ever published.

A cache of arms belonging to a Dutchman had been discovered at the camp. The man was promptly shipped to Auschwitz. But he had a young servant boy, a *pipel* as they were called, a child with a refined and beautiful face, unheard of in the camps. He had the face of a sad angel.

The little servant, like his Dutch master, was cruelly tortured, but would not reveal any information. So the SS sentenced the child to death, along with two other prisoners who had been discovered with arms. Wiesel tells the story:

> One day when we came back from work, we saw three gallows rearing up in the assembly place, three black crows. Roll call. SS all around us; machine guns trained: the traditional ceremony. Three victims in chains—and one of them, the little servant, the sad-eyed angel.
>
> The SS seemed more preoccupied, more disturbed than usual. To hang a young boy in front of thousands of spectators was no light matter. The head of the camp read the verdict. All eyes were on the child. He was lividly pale, almost calm, biting his lips. The gallows threw its shadow over him.
>
> This time the *Lagercapo* refused to act as executioner. Three SS replaced him.
>
> The three victims mounted together onto the chairs.
>
> The three necks were placed at the same moment within the nooses. "Long live liberty!" cried the two adults.
>
> But the child was silent.
>
> "Where is God? Where is He?" someone behind me asked.

Total silence throughout the camp. On the horizon, the sun was setting.

"Bare your heads!" yelled the head of the camp. His voice was raucous. We were weeping.

"Cover your heads!"

Then the march past began. The two adults were no longer alive. Their tongues hung swollen, blue-tinged. But the third rope was still moving; being so light, the child was still alive. . . .

For more than half an hour he stayed there, struggling between life and death, dying in slow agony under our eyes. And we had to look him full in the face. He was still alive when I passed in front of him. His tongue was still red, his eyes were not yet glazed.

Behind me, I heard the same man asking: "Where is God now?" And I heard a voice within me answer him: "Where is He? Here He is—He is hanging here on this gallows. . . ."

That night the soup tasted of corpses.[1]

I don't recall who first brought my attention to this story, but I do remember his comments on it: "Wiesel lost his faith in God at that concentration camp, but not because he quit believing in right and wrong. Far from it. He believed in morality so deeply that he could no longer worship a God who allowed children to be strung up at the gallows and tossed into the ovens."

Had Wiesel understood the voice within him that God was there hanging on the gallows—suffering in and with humanity—and had he known that God was in Christ hanging on the cross, suffering in our place, he need not have lost his faith, but found it.

Nevertheless, in view of such horrible suffering, many of us cannot help asking ourselves a disturbing question: How can *we* continue to believe in such a God?

God Is Captive to a Moral Plan

Part of the answer comes in the fact that God has bound Himself to a moral plan, a plan in which He sometimes delivers His might and glory into captivity.

A *moral* plan? How can a plan be moral which permits indecency, cruelty, and immorality? How can a moral Governor rule and yet fail to reward right and punish evil? If God's holiness demands and rewards righteousness even as it forbids and punishes wickedness, then why doesn't He govern accordingly right now?

Part of the answer is that God's plan involves the permission of sin—its full expression, its final judgment, and its eternal removal. This plan will one day triumph in a new creation of redeemed men and women conformed to Christ and His holiness. One day all things will be set right . . . one day. But not until that day.

Punishment and Reward Not Immediate or Indisputable

Because of this plan, God holds back from fully exercising His power and glory. How satisfying it would be, we think, if God were to publicly reward the righteous and openly punish the wicked. But no. His plan calls for rain to fall on the good and on the evil, for the wheat and the tares to grow together.

But is it a *moral* plan? Yes, moral in that it gives men and women the opportunity to choose the right and shun evil, apart from obvious and compelling immediate gain.

This does not mean that wickedness goes unpunished. God's plan involves appropriate, discernible, but not undeniable judgment and reward.

On a train during the height of World War II, I struck up a conversation with a man skeptical about God. If God really existed, the man said, He ought to use His power to end the war. He ought to reveal Himself clearly and unmistakably. "Why doesn't God write on the sky, 'STOP THIS WAR'?" he demanded.

But God never did exactly what my friend desired. His skywriting took a completely different form—skywriting in the form of American and Allied bombers leveling many of the great cities of Germany.

How can that be called God's skywriting?

Under Hitler, Germany sought to exterminate the Jews. God had promised Abraham and his descendants that He would bless those who blessed the Jews and curse those who cursed them. In response to Nazi atrocities, God did His skywriting with bomb-laden B-17s—an appropriate, discernible, and yet not undeniable judgment. Skeptics could still refuse to see God's hand.

God's universe is so wired that punishment for evil and reward for goodness are built into its natural laws. The circuitry of natural law is such, however, that men are able to deny that the shock of judgment or reward comes from the divine Electrician.

I know something personally about carrying out appropriate retribution (although on a much less serious level!). Years ago I did some wiring to cure our Labrador of his sneaky habit of sleeping in my easy chair after the family had gone to bed.

Morning after morning I would find my chair warm and covered with dog hair. So I wired the chair with an electric fence shocker designed for cattle. About two o'clock in the morning Dutchie yelped, streaked out of the living room, bounded upstairs, and hid under a bed.

He never again trusted that easy chair.

Remembering that story always brings a grin, but at the same time it disturbs me. For if my efforts resulted in such a satisfying result, why does God seem to have such a hard time of it?

I think the answer goes something like this: If every time we sinned we were immediately and unmistakably punished by God, our choice not to repeat the offense would not be moral, but expedient. Similarly, if every time a person did a commendable thing he was instantly rewarded by God, he would likely do the will of God not because it was right, but because it paid.

We might add that God may seem indifferent to moral law because He has delegated to society and to human government its enforcement. And human government, often rebellious against God and dominated by Satan, is allowed to continue to misrule until the cup of its iniquity is filled full before God destroys it.

The Captive God Is in Control

Who was in control when the American embassy in Beirut was bombed?

When hijackers captured a Boeing 727, took its passengers hostage, and killed one of them, who was in charge?

When an American servicemen's center in Italy was bombed, who was in command?

Who is God among the gods in time of tragedy, and why doesn't He step forward and show that He is in control?

Let us return to that fateful day when the Philistines defeated for the second time the armies of Israel and captured the ark of God.

You recall that the presence of the ark of God struck fear into the hearts of Philistia's warriors. They remembered that the LORD had defeated the gods and armies of Egypt. They were afraid! But they steeled themselves, fought, and won.

The sacred account tells the story simply and concisely:

> So the Philistines fought, and the Israelites were defeated and every man fled to his tent. The slaughter was very great; Israel lost thirty thousand foot soldiers. The ark of God was

captured, and Eli's two sons, Hophni and Phinehas, died (1 Samuel 4:10-11).

The slaughter of its armies and the capture of the ark caused Israel once again to cry out in agony and despair. But Eli knew, in part at least, the reason for the defeat. God had warned that he would judge Eli's two wicked sons, whom Eli had failed to restrain. And his daughter-in-law, dying in childbirth, named her son Ichabod, saying, "The glory has departed from Israel" (1 Samuel 4:21).

We cannot fathom the depths of Israel's despair. Private tragedy involving the unexpected loss of a loved one might give us some hint. But it could never duplicate the intensity and perplexity of this national tragedy. In a single day some thirty thousand Israeli soldiers died in battle. No wonder the weeping was great!

The Philistines Celebrate

In contrast to the gloom that settled over Israel, all Philistia must have rejoiced at the victory and the capture of the ark of God. The ark was brought into the house of Dagon and set up before the idol. *His captive!*

All heathendom broke loose that night. If there is such a thing as rejoicing among the fallen angels, they must have done so that night. The triumphant shouts of giddy Philistines could be heard all night long.

Hours passed, the next morning dawned, and with it a shock. The incredible had occurred. The rumor tore through Philistia like wildfire: "It can't be true—can it?" But there was no denying it. The report was verified and spread.

Dagon was on his face before the ark of God!

If traumatic shock can bring the drunken to sobriety, then thousands in Philistia awoke to the sober reality that Dagon was down—down on his face before the LORD.

Perhaps there was some mistake? An earthquake?
And so "they took Dagon and put him back in his place"
(1 Samuel 5:3). It could not happen like this again!

They were right. The second time it was worse:
"The following morning when they rose, there was
Dagon, fallen on his face on the ground before the ark of
the LORD! His head and hands had been broken off and
were lying on the threshold; only his body remained" (1
Samuel 5:4).

The Captive God Works the Night Shift

The dawn that brought dismay to Philistia and joy to
Israel revealed that the captive God had been working in
the night, overcoming the power of darkness (Colossians
1:13).

I have suggested that this story illustrates God's
method of working in the world. He works in enemy territory, where Satan is called prince and god. God's labor
is often not obvious, overwhelming, of the twelve-legions-
of-angels variety. Rather, he quietly gathers disciples to
salvation, truth, and righteousness—not by lightning,
thunder, and earthquake, but by the still, small voice of
Spirit-wrought conviction.

God works as an undercover agent, a representative
of a government in exile. We are his ambassadors . . .
and our embassies are frequently assaulted.

How Does God Work as a Captive?

The working of God in the house of Dagon, and
subsequently in Philistia, suggests some things about the
way He customarily works in today's world.

1. God is pictured as working in the devil's territory.

Several Scriptures mark out this world as Satan's
domain. He is called the god of this age, the ruler of the
world, and the prince of the power of the air (2
Corinthians 4:4; John 12:31, 14:30, 16:11; Ephesians 2:2).

Satan offered to give Jesus the kingdoms of the world if our Lord would fall down and worship him (Matthew 4:8-9). The devil's man, called the man of sin and the son of perdition, will exalt himself above God and receive worship as God (2 Thessalonians 2:3-4, KJV).

2. *It was Israel's sin that put God's presence in the house of Dagon.*

Detestable, idolatrous sin moved God to forsake the tabernacle at Shiloh and to deliver his strength into captivity and his glory into the enemy's hands. Adam's sin preceded that of Israel, and ours has followed. Together we have made the world "a house of Dagon." It is alienated to such a degree that when Jesus "came to that which was his own, his own did not receive him" (John 1:11).

3. *God's purpose in going to the house of Dagon was redemptive.*

God's purpose was to expose Dagon as a fraud, convict the Philistines of their sin, and confirm that the LORD was indeed the covenant-keeping God of Abraham, Isaac, and Jacob.

4. *The humiliation of Dagon involved two acts of divine judgment.*

Dagon fell down before the ark of God the first night of the ark's captivity. Propped in place once more, he failed to stay on his feet for the second round. The priests of Dagon found him the following morning on his face once again, with his head broken off and his hands severed from his arms.

Likewise, Satan's head was bruised when Christ was crucified (Genesis 3:15) and when Jesus comes to reign over the whole world, he will utterly defeat and eventually destroy the evil one (Revelation 19:11-20:10).

5. *God's encounter with Dagon was but one of many of His encounters with the gods of this world.*

Like Rachel, who stole the household gods of her father Laban, the children of Israel repeatedly took the gods of the surrounding nations and exalted them above the LORD: "They forsook the LORD, the God of their fathers . . . [and] followed and worshiped various gods of the peoples around them" (Judges 2:12). Like children who say, "My dad can lick your dad," so ancient nations proclaimed the superiority of their gods over the god of those they conquered. Sometimes, the true God demonstrated He alone was God by giving Israel military victory where it seemed humanly impossible.

So it was that God delivered the invading hordes of Ben-Hadad, king of Syria, into the hands of wicked king Ahab of Israel. He did so, that Ahab and Israel would know that the LORD was God (1 Kings 20:13). The servants of the king of Syria ascribed their defeat to the gods of Israel, whom they thought to be gods of the hills. They reasoned that they could defeat the armies of Israel if they fought them on the plains. So in the spring of the year, Ben-Hadad mustered his vast army against Israel outside the territory of her gods.

> The Israelites camped opposite them like two small flocks of goats, while the Arameans covered the countryside. The man of God came up and told the king of Israel, "This is what the LORD says: 'Because the Arameans think the LORD is a god of the hills and not a god of the valleys, I will deliver this vast army into your hands, and you will know that I am the LORD' " (1 Kings 20:27-28).

Conversely, Ahaz, king of Judah, sacrificed to the gods of Damascus which had defeated him. He reasoned, "Since the gods of the kings of Aram have helped them, I will sacrifice to them so they will help me" (2 Chronicles 28:23).

Earl Dix, a missionary serving in Zaire, Africa, until his recent retirement and death, was warned by a local tribal chief that unless he offered sacrifice to the god of Pangba, a beautiful water hole in the tall grass country, his hunting would be unsuccessful. The sacrifice didn't have to be much—any old thing of little or no value—but without it he would hunt in vain.

Earl countered that his God was a jealous God and he could not sacrifice to another. In spite of warnings that he would come back with nothing, Earl set out for the water hole with his guides, porters, and .25 caliber Winchester.

He missed two easy shots, and it looked like the god of Pangba had things under his control. Earl's guides left him and went back to their village. After hours of waiting, near sundown Earl crawled his way into the midst of a herd of eleven gazelles and shot all eleven of them. Somehow, they did not spook as expected. His porters gathered them up and carried them back to the village. On the way Earl saw and killed three waterbucks.

An excited African came with news that a huge hippopotamus was feeding in a nearby river. It was added to the kill, even though a .25 caliber Winchester is hardly the gun for such big game.

The meat from Earl's miraculous hunting expedition supplied for many days the needs of his safari group and of the village where they were staying. What could not be used immediately was smoked and preserved for later use.

Such contests between the Lord God omnipotent and the tribal gods of satanic or human fabrication find their counterparts in our modern world.

Our pluralistic society prostrates itself before gods old and new—gods from Buddha to Baghwan, from Baal and Ashtoreth to Sexual Liberation. And in our temples of learning, the gods of science, of evolution, of mechanistic psychology, and of man-exalting humanism call for worship. In the battle for the human soul the glory and power of God as seen in creation have been taken captive by the satanic blindness which ascribes all the marvels of creation to chance. These false gods hold captive the God of the Bible as did the devotees of Dagon—not knowing that a night of destruction lies ahead.

   6. Defeated and discouraged Israel did not know what God was doing while the ark remained captive in the house of Dagon.

   How often is this the case with us? It was so with Habakkuk, many years after the capture of the ark. The prophet could not understand the triumph of evil in his day. So he asked God a question:

> How long, O LORD, must I call for help,
>   but you do not listen?
> Or cry out to you, "Violence!"
>   but you do not save?
> Why do you make me look at injustice?
>   Why do you tolerate wrong?
> Destruction and violence are before me;
>   there is strife, and conflict abounds.
> Therefore the law is paralyzed,
>   and justice never prevails.
> The wicked hem in the righteous,
>   so that justice is perverted (Habakkuk 1:2-4).

   What was God's answer to the prophet? Was God really so indifferent to the reign of wickedness and violence in Israel? No. His answer, in effect: "I *am* working. I am doing something about it" (see Habakkuk 1:5).

   As helpful as these six comparisons might be, however, we must recognize that they fail in one important respect: the time involved. On the second day of His captivity God destroyed the idol Dagon, and in seven months His plagues upon Philistia caused the Philistines to plead for deliverance. God's providences in most of history have not brought judgment and relief so soon or so fast.

God's Differing Roles

God works in this world in two different roles. First, He works as the almighty God, sovereign in providential control over the rise and fall of nations. Second, He works in the role of a captive God. In a later chapter we call this the over/under principle.

God told Habakkuk that He would use the savage Babylonians to punish unrepentant Israel. Under Nebuchadnezzar they invaded the land, captured Jerusalem, sacked and looted the temple, killed uncounted numbers of Jews, and led many thousands of others into distant captivity. This was the work of God in keeping with His promise, "I am raising up the Babylonians" (Habakkuk 1:6).

As part of God's promise to Abraham that his descendants should be a blessing to all the earth, God appointed Israel to be an instrument of His wrath and judgment against the wicked nations of Canaan. Judgment fell when God determined that these nations had filled full their cup of iniquity. But Israel failed to fully carry out God's judgment and became infected with Canaanite sins and diseases, worshiped their gods, and departed from worshiping and serving the Lord. Consequently, God used the conquering Babylonians to chasten His chosen but unrepentant people.

In his second role, God appears to work as a captive God. The enemy overruns the land of covenant promise, the temple is looted and destroyed, and His people are carried away into captivity—proof enough (to many observers) that enemy gods were stronger than the God of Israel. In His role as a captive God, the Lord Himself went into captivity with His people. In the words of Ezekiel 11:16, God promised to be a refuge for His scattered sons and daughters:

> Thus saith the Lord GOD; Although I have cast
> them far off among the heathen, and although

I have scattered them among the countries, yet will I be to them as a little sanctuary in the countries where they shall come (KJV).

The Value of Sanctuary

Our once-upon-a-time Australian cattle dog, Sydney, learned the value of sanctuary. One day Sydney accompanied me in my pickup to a farm where I loaded up some lumber from alder logs sawed by a portable sawmill. The mill was in a pasture surrounded by an electric fence. When I got out of the truck to open the gate, Sydney got out to explore the place.

A few minutes later as I backed the truck toward the stacked lumber, I noticed Sydney was frantically trying to crawl under the truck. Fortunately I did not run over him. I stopped the truck, opened the door, and in bounded Sydney. He refused to leave his sanctuary the whole time we were there. He had run into the electric fence, and it scared the daylights out of him.

We came back a week later. Sydney remembered his ordeal and refused to leave the safety of the pickup's cab. It was a little sanctuary for him. He was a dog with real horse sense.

And back in Babylon, faithful Israelites such as Daniel, Shadrach, Meshach, and Abednego proved that the "captive" God, their sanctuary, was in control after all.

Who was in control when the American embassy was bombed and marines killed? Who was in control when the TWA jetliner was taken hostage or the American servicemen's center bombed?

Ultimately, God was. Either directly or through intermediaries, God is always in control. He raised up the Babylonians to punish Israel, and today (for reasons of His own) He continues to permit evil which He hates and forbids. He pleads with us as He pled with Israel: "Do not do this detestable thing which I hate!" (Jeremiah 44:4).

When we think of American humiliation and tragedy at the hands of her enemies, could it be that God is warning us to turn away from the increasing godlessness and immorality in our once-enlightened nation?

As over against God's ultimate control, Satan and man exercise a contingent, temporary control. So it was when God delivered his Son to die and the rulers of Israel and Rome took Him and by wicked hands crucified Him. So it is when embassies and servicemen's centers are bombed, and boats and planes hijacked.

Sometimes those who highlight the sovereignty of God plead for us to "Let God be God." We really don't need to worry about that, for God can well take care of Himself. Nevertheless, He who rules over the hosts of the heavens calls upon us to pray that His will be done on earth as it is in heaven. And in so doing He limits His workings. Such is the limitation God has placed upon Himself.

I have called it His "operational restraint." Operational restraint is having the atom bomb and not using it.

God is fighting—and winning, all appearances to the contrary—the war against Satan and sin. He is using the "conventional weapons" of moral and spiritual warfare rather than blinding and pulverizing bursts of irresistible power.

God *will* win the war. It is certain. But in the meanwhile, before the heat of the last battle cools, there will be casualties. Casualties in the form of battered and torn bodies. Casualties in the form of bruised and shaken faiths. Casualties in the form of agonized pleas for the General's help that seem to go unheeded. Casualties in the form of unanswered questions.

It is to some of those casualties that we now turn.

Chapter 3, Notes

1. Elie Wiesel, *Night* (New York: Bantam, 1982), p. 75-76.

CHAPTER 4

God, Where Have You Been?

An unusual ache. An appointment with the doctor. Tests. Waiting. A phone call. Tears.

"God, where have You been?"

How often that cry bursts from the lips of God's children! Excruciating pain or overwhelming temptations trample our nicely ordered lives, and suddenly such questions are everywhere.

"God, where have You been?"

It was that way many years ago with a young student at Multnomah School of the Bible. She developed an infection in her knee which proved to be cancer. We prayed for her healing.

Her leg was cut off at the knee.

Later the cancer appeared in her hip joint. The whole school joined in prayer that the hip be spared.

Her leg was removed at the hip.

The cancer continued to spread. We prayed.

She died.

"God, where have You been? Why have You not answered? Why have You not spared?"

The questions came. The answers didn't.

In this case, the substitute answer to prayer made this girl, Dorothy Angerstein, a vibrant Christian witness to the whole hospital. Our heavenly Father gave Himself to her in abounding measure. Knowing how to give the Best Gift, infinitely better than the finest gifts a human father gives his son, God promised to give His Holy Spirit—Himself—to those who ask Him (Luke 11:13).

But not everyone enjoys such assurance and peace. Certainly not Israel when it suffered defeat at the hands of the Philistines and lost four thousand men in battle. Its elders raised the cry, "Why did the LORD bring defeat upon us today before the Philistines?" (1 Samuel 4:3).

Perhaps remembering the victory at Jericho when the ark of God led the armies of Israel, the elders sent for the ark, hoping that it would save them from the hands of the enemy. And when the Philistines learned that the ark had come into the camp of Israel, they feared greatly and cried out, "A god has come into the camp." They, too, remembered His mighty workings when He delivered the Israelites from slavery in Egypt.

Both Hebrew and Philistine counted upon the presence of God in the ark—the Hebrew trusting hopefully, the Philistine fearing.

But when the ark was taken captive, Israel could well question, "God, where were You?"

Long before them, Adam and Eve could have asked the same question.

Their sin had made their paradise a place of fear and remorse. The pleasant fruits of every tree which God had given them called to mind what might have been. The forbidden fruit that would make them as gods already had become bitter to their taste. They knew they were naked. They tried to cover themselves and to hide from God.

It didn't work. The LORD came into the Garden in the cool of the day and called to Adam, "Where are you?"

Adam, seeking to lay the blame on shoulders other than his own, might have replied, "Where have *You* been? Where were You when the serpent came to beguile us? Why were we not warned?"

Adam isn't alone. Haven't we asked similar questions when we have been tempted and failed? Haven't we accused God by saying, "God, where have You been?"

The Whereabouts of God and Man

Where is God? Where is man? Dare we presume to answer those questions? Could it be that the whereabouts of God and of man must be found in the wilderness of free will and of shared sovereignty? Sometimes a howling wilderness. Again, a barren waste. A place of thirst, hunger, monotony. No "leeks and garlics" (for those hankering for such). But also a place of hills and valleys, of springs and an occasional oasis. For God is a God of both the mountains and the valleys—of the ups and downs of life.

Our wilderness wanderings in the hills and valleys of moral choice sometimes enthrall us with vistas of far-off promised lands, or again find us grumbling about the scarcity of water or about our bland and monotonous diet of manna.

Our wilderness wanderings have not always been led by the cloud by day and the pillar of fire by night. In that wilderness, God is asking, "Where are you?" And in our lostness, failure, and frustration, we reply, "God, where have *You* been?"

God's purpose in placing us in the wilderness is to know our hearts (Deuteronomy 8:2). The palpable presence of Satan and the seeming absence of God in the Garden of Eden foreshadowed the circumstances in the ensuing world in which moral choices must be made. Out of it God secured a new creation whose free moral choices would crystallize into perfect conformity to Jesus Christ.

That is a large order, involving our redemption and the renewal of the divine image in us.

Does God Hide Himself?

That God hides Himself is a truth and complaint often voiced in Scripture. Isaiah 45:15 states it categorically: "Truly you are a God who hides himself." The psalmists and Job question the why and the wherefore of God's hiding: "Why, O LORD, do you stand far off? Why do you hide yourself in times of trouble?" (Psalm 10:1; see also Psalm 44:24, 88:14, 104:29). "Why do you hide your face and consider me your enemy?" (Job 13:24). Isaiah says that Israel's sins hid God's face from them (Isaiah 59:2), but Job's experience was a test of his righteousness and faith.

In either case, hiding served God's purpose. It judged sinners and tested saints.

The God who hides Himself, but is seen by the eye of faith, is the God of the manger, wrapped in swaddling clothes, and the God of the cross, stripped of His robe.

He is also God of the throne and the scepter, glorious in majesty and power. But His coming glory is now seen in the rising and setting of the sun, the balancing of the clouds; in the pounding of the surf; in the mountains and lakes, trees and flowers; and in the radiance of lives transformed by the Spirit of God.

The Tapestry of Faith

The tapestry of faith, woven by man and God out of the visible and invisible worlds, lies open in its construction and beauty in Hebrews 11. Faith is there defined in terms of "assurance" of things hoped for and "conviction" concerning things not seen (NASB). The *assurance* may well be confidence supported by evidence and may stem from man's search for God and finding Him in nature, in His word, in the Incarnation, and at the cross. God's part in the development of faith is to give enlightenment, or *conviction*, through the Holy Spirit concerning things not seen. It means spiritual perception of the invisible things of God.

To make possible moral choices made by faith—with viable options between God and mammon, between blessing and cursing, life or death—God cannot be overpoweringly, gloriously present. The supreme object of our faith, unlike the pleasures of time and sensation, remains hidden. Luther put it this way: "That there may be room for faith . . . all that is believed must be hidden."[1] It is like a hard-shelled black walnut, its pulpy outer husk rotted and ready to stain hands dark brown, yet with an inner shell shielding a delicious nut. To get to the nut, you must crack the inner shell with a heavy hammer blow.

Jesus often presented Himself and His parables as something like the outer shell of that black walnut. The Syrophoenecian woman found this out. She heard about Him, came and fell at His feet, and begged Him to cast a demon out of her daughter.

Jesus replied with seeming hard-shelled brusqueness, "First let the children eat all they want . . . for it is not right to take the children's bread and toss it to their dogs" (Mark 7:27).

Undaunted, and by faith taking her place as a Gentile "dog," she replied, "Yes, Lord . . . but even the dogs under the table eat the children's crumbs." Her faith penetrated the seeming dark and forbidding husk of cultural racism and touched the tender heart of Jesus. Her child was healed, her faith rewarded. But she had to *choose* to place herself in Jesus' care.

Does Man's Choice of God Mean Much to Him?

When God created angels and men with free moral agency, I believe He wanted more than anything else the fellowship and loving service of those who would freely choose Him. In order that man's choices should be uncoerced and free, God has limited the manner and frequency of His appearances. He has become captive to His own wise plan.

But under what conditions are free moral choices made? It is to that question that we now turn.

How Moral Choices Are Made

Free choices can be made only by personal beings with the ability to reason, to feel, and to make decisions. This was a part of the image of God in which man was created.

The exercise of moral choice requires that there be situations featuring options both good and bad, right and wrong; or, as in the Garden of Eden, prohibited and permitted.

Free moral choice can take place ideally only in the absence of compulsion. First Corinthians 7:37 gives a picture of ideal freedom. It is he "who has settled the matter in his own mind, who is under no compulsion but has control over his own will." If man is compelled to choose by his own nature or character, by God or by Satan, or by something or somebody else, choice is not truly or ideally free.

We thank God the human spirit can and does choose to do right in spite of compulsion to do the opposite. Attempts to break man's resolve to do right by promises of power and pleasure or by fiendish torture have often failed. In the history of mankind's struggle for freedom, millions have died as martyrs rather than compromise their character and their cause.

Man is not truly free if he is no more than a biochemical mechanism whose choices are determined by the psychological and physical forces playing upon him.

If a man is compelled to choose in line with his nature, disposition, and character, then he is not free.

His disposition compels him. It is true that we make decisions normally in line with our basic disposition. In the words of our Lord, "Out of the overflow of the heart the mouth speaks. The good man brings good things out of the good stored up in him, and the evil man brings evil things out of the evil stored up in him" (Matthew 12:34, 35). This is in line with the law of sowing and reaping. It is the principle upon which character is formed, and contains both good news and bad news.

The good news is that right choices made out of the good treasure of the heart tend to form and strengthen good character.

The bad news is that wrong choices contribute to solidifying character in the form of evil.

I am profoundly thankful that individual choices normally arise out of and conform to the central bent or disposition of the will. But I am equally grateful that there is no dispositional compulsion by which choices are necessarily determined by character.

Man Is Not without Choice

If individual choices were determined by the character of the individual, then Adam, created with a holy nature, could not have sinned. And fallen man, with his sin nature, would be incapable of responding to God.

But Adam, we are told, had a two-directional freedom. He was free to obey God or to disobey. Not so if freedom consists of making choices solely in accordance with one's nature. Since Adam was holy by nature, he acted "out of character" and denied himself when he disobeyed God.

Is modern man different than Adam? It is said fallen man has only a one-dimensional freedom. He is free only to sin, and he does that freely because it is in line with and arises out of his sin nature. While insisting that man is free in his sin because he wants to sin, yet it is commonly maintained that such freedom to sin is an enslavement of the will which prohibits a man from turning to God. In Luther's metaphor, man is a beast, both God and Satan want to ride him, and man has no choice as to who sits on his back.

Can We Make Choices Contrary to Our Nature?

Must we always choose in line with our disposition? Adam fell below his created perfection, and fallen man can rise above his sinful nature. In both the fall and in the restoration of man, a second party is involved. In the fall, it was Satan deceiving and blinding; in the restoration it is God—*must be God*—opening blind eyes and renewing the will.

Man's fall was by faith and his restoration is by faith, and faith that comes by hearing. Adam listened to Satan, and faith in his alluring lie came by hearing. By hearing and giving heed to the word of God fallen man is given saving faith.

In his conversion, man justifies God in His judgment against sin, repents of sin, denies himself—in part by choosing to believe God contrary to his fallen nature—and puts his faith in the Lord Jesus Christ. Man's decision to obey the gospel and to receive Christ as Savior is indeed made in man's highest self-interest, but it is also a moral choice in which he justifies God in His righteous judgment against sin. He repents and believes because it is the right thing to do (Luke 7:29; see also Exodus 9:27).

God's Glory Would Control Our Choices

The freedom to accept or to reject the will of God must take place where God is not manifestly, dazzlingly present. Had God appeared in the Garden of Eden in awesome presence as He appeared to the prophet Isaiah, He would have controlled Adam's choice by sheer force of glory. Adam would have fallen prostrate before God. The apostle John, who saw the glorified Son of Man, "fell at his feet as though dead" (Revelation 1:17).

Perhaps at one time or another you have cruised down the highway faster than the speed limit. Fortunately, you saw the flashing lights of a patrol car alongside the highway, parked beside a victim. Automatically your foot lifted from the accelerator and you slid past the patrolman well under the speed limit. But as the flashing lights grew smaller and dimmer in your rear view mirror, you resumed your speed. Your attitude toward the speed law was controlled by catching a glimpse of the patrolman. Had he followed, you would have obeyed the law.

Such an assumption was supported recently by an article in the *Jerusalem Post*. After twenty people were killed in one week on Israeli roads, Transport Minister Haim Corfu is reported to have said, "We believe that a visible police presence on the road will go a long way in changing driving habits."

If God had appeared in the Garden in glorious and awesome presence, Adam would not have fallen. But God, like Paul in writing to the Philippian believers, wanted obedience not in His presence only, but also in His absence. God did not want to compel the choice to obey.

God wants to know how we will act in His absence. That is what the sacred writer says in describing how Hezekiah, king of Judah, displayed all his wealth and splendor to certain ambassadors from Babylon: "God left him to test him and to know everything that was in his heart" (2 Chronicles 32:31).

And so it was in the case of the nobleman who left for a distant country to receive for himself a kingdom and later to return (Luke 19:12). His absence was planned.

God Did Not Abandon Adam and Eve

Did God really abandon Adam and Eve? As we reflect upon it, we see that God did not leave them completely alone. He has never left Himself without a witness (Acts 14:17).

God's presence was made known to them in the beauty and fruitfulness of the Garden of Eden. Its fabulous fruits provided nourishment and enjoyment. They could eat of every tree of the Garden but one, and they clearly remembered that God had warned them on pain of death not to eat of the tree of the knowledge of good and evil.

And was not God also present in some way through His word? Jesus spoke of His words as being spirit and life, and the writer to the Hebrews called the word of God "living and active. Sharper than any double-edged sword . . . " (Hebrews 4:12).

And God was present in His image in Adam and Eve. Fresh from the creative hand of God, complete and satisfied in their composite reflection of His image, their godlike qualities should have been a constant reminder of God's reality and presence.

I know of no record in Scripture that God had revealed to Adam and Eve an account of Satan's rebellion. There was no explicit warning against the deceiver. But God commissioned Adam to tend and *keep*, or *guard*, the Garden. This job description could have been a warning that the Garden would be invaded. Furthermore, naming one tree "the tree of the knowledge of good and evil" could also have warned that evil existed and should be avoided.

Life-Changing Choices Made by Faith

Whether in the Garden or in the moral wilderness of fallen humanity, life-shaping choices are made by faith. Such faith may be in God, in one's self, or in Satan. The object of faith may be worthy of faith or unworthy. Somehow, Adam and Eve failed to see the invisible God in His visible handiwork in the Garden and in His word written in their hearts. While they took His name upon their lips, the consciousness of His presence was eclipsed by the brilliance of the false angel of light. They tolerated his questioning of God, then embraced his denial of Him. They believed Satan rather than God.

From the standpoint of the physical, God remains invisible and absent. But spiritual perception sees the invisible things of God in the things that are seen, in the words of Romans 1:20, even His eternal power and godhead. In His plan for a moral universe, where choice is not to be compelled by the irresistible brightness of the Light unapproachable, God has been pleased to operate as the invisible, hidden God, yet seen in His creative power and providence.

But the things that are seen must be interpreted.

Does the world with its countless forms of life constitute evidence of creation? Or of chance working by evolution?

How do we understand war, famine, pestilence, and death?

What does a volcanic eruption which kills twenty or thirty thousand people say about God?

What does the AIDS virus tell us? Many would vehemently deny that such a thing as AIDS could be caused or permitted by a loving God. In the words of the Philistines, whose cities were being plagued by the presence of God in the ark of the covenant, those who deny God's providential judgment say in effect, "It happened to us by chance" (1 Samuel 6:9).

Natural Law Has No Favorites

An environment where moral choices are made must be a place where natural law operates impartially.

For example, gravity uniformly pulls objects toward the earth. Anyone, sinner or saint, who loses his foothold and falls from a height, crashes to the ground.

Once I was using a chain saw to cut off the limbs of a large fir tree. I climbed the tree about twenty-five feet, then descended, cutting off branches as I came down. Some were four or five inches in diameter. As I continued to cut, some of the branches piled up on the limb which supported me. Suddenly my limb broke off . . . and left me to the law of gravity, with a running chain saw in my hands. Fortunately my fall was broken by branches under me, I tossed away the saw, and landed without injury.

It has been said there are no accidents with God, but there are with men, and some are more accident-prone than others. Moreover, damaging accidents may seemingly "just happen" or may result from careless violation of a natural law or from the teeth and jaws of machines designed to cut or crush. Shop saws designed for sawing wood will also cut fingers. Axes split wood and human flesh—sanctified flesh, too. Men are destined to die once; all men, not just the wicked.

Suppose that natural law was administered in such a way that Christians were exempted from the harmful consequences of violating it.

Suppose they could overeat without getting fat or sick, drink without getting drunk, smoke and escape the hazards of lung cancer and heart attack, speed and not risk accident.

In short, suppose Christians became an "elect exception" to the universal principle that a man reaps what he sows. They would constitute a here-and-now privileged class, a sort of elite, private club. To join such a club would be considered, like honesty, the best policy. But the decision to join would be expedient rather than moral. Choosing Christ is expedient *and* moral.

In the next chapter we shall seek to more fully understand how this is so.

Chapter 4, Notes

1. Martin Luther, *The Bondage of the Will,* trans. J.I. Packer and O. R. Johnston (Old Tappan, N.J.: Fleming H. Revell, 1970).

CHAPTER 5

Freedom within the Grace of God

IN the little backwoods, funny-paper community of "Lil' Abner," there lived an excess of widows and a scarcity of bachelors willing to say "I do." Each year on what was called "Sadie Hawkins Day," bachelors were up for grabs. But there were rules.

At the firing of a starting gun, frightened and miserable bachelors ran for their lives and freedom. Shortly thereafter, widows were unleashed and thundered in pursuit of their hapless victims. Those caught were dragged back to the starting line and joined in holy wedlock. And I presume they lived happily ever after—even the bachelors.

Why do I tell this little story? It's because God's grace in saving us is widely represented in terms akin to Sadie Hawkins Day. Miserable bachelor-sinners are running away from God as fast as they can. They are caught by irresistible grace and dragged back to the "marrying up" line. Now born again, they believe. They have been blessed by "loving violence."

What bothers me about all this is that there is more at stake than the capture of individual bachelors.

For God in sovereign grace to save one soul and not another, and to do so without the prior consenting faith of the sinner would indeed be a triumph of sovereign grace. But would it be at the expense of the moral victory of a free choice to repent, believe, and obey God?

Three Questions

Thinking of salvation and free choice and God's will immediately brings three prominent questions to mind:

- Is man really able or free to choose God and salvation?

- Would such a choice be a moral choice and a moral victory for God?

- Would such a free choice add more to the glory and satisfaction of God than for Him to save us through sovereign, irresistible grace?

Please know that I affirm freedom within the grace of God, not free will apart from the grace of God. I am saying that since "the grace of God that brings salvation has appeared to all men" (Titus 2:11), man is able to respond to Christ's invitation to come to Him. He is responsible to obey the gospel and by grace he is *response able.*

Scripture frequently represents man as captive to Satan and a slave to sin. Some theologians add that his will is so enslaved that he cannot turn to God. But enslavement does not always imply bondage of the will. It took enslavement and cruel bondage in Egypt to give the children of Israel the will to seek release.

The wives of David and of his men must have longed for release more than anything else when they were taken captive by their enemies. Jesus came to proclaim liberty to the captives (Isaiah 61:1, KJV), and He does so on the ground that through His death He has broken the power of Satan (Hebrews 2:14-15).

Bondage to Sin

I would never minimize the reality and awfulness of man's slavery to sin and Satan. It involves intellectual and spiritual darkness, moral degradation, and enslavement of the will to do evil. The god of this world has blinded the minds of those who do not believe (2 Corinthians 4:4). They call evil good, and good evil (Isaiah 5:20), and they cannot amend their evil ways (Romans 7:18). Man in this condition is free only in the sense that he makes choices in line with his darkened intellect. He chooses to do evil.

When I say, "We are free," it seems I have forgotten that many are Satan's captives, bound by sinful habits; that others are under chains of grinding poverty; that whole nations are virtual slaves to godless government; and that countless millions have been dehumanized in slave labor camps.

But I haven't forgotten. I remember the Cuban general who was imprisoned, tortured, and debased by Castro for some twenty years. He could not be broken. His spirit refused to be coerced.

Then there is Aleksandr Solzhenitsyn who thanks God that he found liberty—highest freedom—in his spirit while in the Russian gulag.

I am talking about freedom in Satan's world invaded by the grace of God.

Freedom of the will has been variously defined. It is said to be the power of contrary choice, the ability to choose good or evil. No, say others, freedom is choosing in line with one's nature. So in the case of fallen man, his ultimate choices can only be self-centered and evil.

Freedom Defined

I am proposing that freedom consists in the power to choose a course of action in line with what is perceived

to be good or in one's best interests. It may involve willing and acting contrary to one's central disposition or
nature, and in that case amounts to denying oneself.
Here I am following the teaching of Jesus regarding disci-
pleship. In addressing both His disciples and the multi-
tude, presumably many unsaved among them, He said,
"Whosoever will come after me, let him deny himself,
and take up his cross, and follow me" (Mark 8:34, KJV;
see also Matthew 16:24, Luke 9:23).

If such a decision can be made only through
enabling grace, remember that I am writing of freedom
within grace, not freedom opposed to grace. The decision to deny oneself, to choose contrary to nature, is a
crisis decision—conversion—involving repentance and
faith.

In a world where the grace of God has appeared,
where the Son came and died for our sins, where the
Spirit has come and is convicting the world of sin, righteousness, and judgment, in such a world—our
world—man is able, or *has available ability*, to obey the
gospel.

The basic ingredient in freedom is the ability to
deny oneself. We *can* choose contrary to our nature.
While choices are ordinarily in line with one's central
desire and disposition, these can be denied. Remember
that Adam denied his holy nature when he sinned.

Choice According to Perception

Self-affirmation in choosing evil or self-denial in
choosing good arises out of our perception of what is
good. Eve was deceived and made a wrong choice contrary to her holy nature when she saw that the forbidden
fruit was good for food, pleasing to the eye, and desirable
for gaining wisdom. She denied her holy nature because
she had a wrong perception of what was good for her.

According to Isaiah 5:20, there are those who
perceive that evil is good and good is evil—and there are

a lot of such folk around today. They freely make wrong choices because of a darkened perception.

The good news is that perceptions can be changed. The understanding can be enlightened by the power of the Holy Spirit so that right choices, including the supreme choice to obey the gospel, can be made by fallen man. *We can deny ourselves.* Or to put it another way, as did the prodigal son, man can "come to himself"—see himself as a son, not a swineherd (see also 2 Chronicles 6:37).

Changed perception and faith come by hearing. Adam and Eve listened to Satan, and in hearing his lie, their understanding was darkened and they placed their faith in him. They denied themselves and acted out of a false perception of what was good.

Fallen man's darkened understanding and wrong perception of God and salvation can be changed, and repentance toward God and faith in our Lord Jesus Christ can be imparted by hearing the word of God (Romans 10:17). The entrance of God's word gives light. The holy Scriptures are able to make us wise unto salvation. The truth can set us free.

We enter into the glorious liberty of the children of God by grace through faith. Saving faith comes by hearing, and hearing by the word of God. Such faith in God's truth can change our perception of God, of sin, and of salvation, and can cause us to perceive and to choose God's will as our highest good.

As evangelical Christians, we unite in praising God because He saved us by grace through faith. Apart from the atoning sacrifice of Christ and the enlightening and convicting work of the Holy Spirit, no one could or would be saved. Boasting is eliminated. God is worthy of all worship and praise because of His victory over sin and death.

It seems to me that in our zeal to magnify the grace of God in saving lost and rebellious men, emphasizing that it is all of God, we forget that God has high stakes in another victory. It is the victory of winning the free moral choice of His creatures.

God will ultimately rejoice over obedient Israel and all the redeemed as predicted in Deuteronomy 30:9-10: " . . . The LORD will again delight in you and make you prosperous, just as he delighted in your fathers, if you obey the LORD your God. . . ."

Not all the angels followed Satan in a perverted exercise of freedom. An innumerable company made right decisions and became the heavenly host which delights to do the will of God.

Can Fallen Man Make a Right Decision?

Could it be that fallen man, participant and victim in Adam's fatal decision, can by the grace of God make a right decision to the glory of God? Or, if man is but the passive recipient of overmastering grace, then has God lost in the battle with Satan over the free will of man?

Wasn't the whole business of creating angels and men as free moral agents brought about because God wanted such to worship Him? In the struggle between God and Satan over Job, did not Satan say that man would not choose to serve God if he could get away with it?

If grace is indeed irresistible, wherein lies the moral victory for God?

This is not to say that man doesn't need the gracious, enlightening, convicting work of the Spirit of God; but it is to say that when this work of God is done, man then must have a change of mind toward God and personally and freely receive Him as Savior.

According to Acts 5:31 and 11:18, God *has given* the gift of repentance both to the Jews and to the Gentiles. How this gracious gift relates to human responsibility is beautifully expressed by Terry in his *Biblical Dogmatics.* He says:

But if it [repentance] be a gift of God, some one will ask why, then, man should be called on to repent and turn to God. The matter explains itself when we keep in mind the doctrine of sin as already described. There can be no genuine repentance in the soul without an antecedent conviction of sin by the revealing law and Spirit of God. In thinking of repentance as God's gift, we have in mind the indispensable gracious conditions which lead to repentance. God first flashed light upon the darkened understanding; He reveals the knowledge of sin, and by the working of the Holy Spirit begets a longing for deliverance from sin. All this is the necessary preliminary to a godly sorrow for sin, and may well be spoken of as the gift of God. But when all this work of conviction is wrought in the heart, it yet remains for the conscious soul with its own freedom of will to respond to such calls to repentance as found in Matt. 3:2, 8; 4:17; Mk. 1:15; Lk. 13:3, 5; Acts 2:38; 3:19; 8:22.[1]

From the point of view of victory for God over Satan in the battle for the wills of men, Job seems to have more than made up for the defeat of Adam. I am speaking of the personal victory of Job, not of consequences to the race. Adam fell from his position of created holiness while freely enjoying the fruits of paradise. Job maintained his integrity, despite the loss of family, wealth, honor, and health, and said, "Though he slay me, yet will I trust Him." This was a great victory both for Job and for God, and it must have gladdened our Lord's heart!

Is Man's Choice of God a Moral Victory for God?

And now to the second question: Would man's choice to obey God and gospel, while expedient and in line with man's highest self-interest, be a moral choice also, and hence a moral victory for God?

I assume that biblical morality is being and doing what is right as this is revealed in the word of God. But it may be argued that to believe the gospel in order to escape the sufferings of hell is expedient and selfish, not moral. Hence man's response to God in obeying the gospel adds nothing to God's victory over Satan in the area of free will. But such is not the case.

Obviously, obedience to the will of God is moral as well as expedient. And since it is the will of God for men to choose life, it is moral to do so. When Moses spoke for God in giving the law to Israel, he said, "I have set before you life and death, blessings and curses. Now choose life, so that you and your children may live" (Deuteronomy 30:19).

Interestingly enough, primitive morality, according to a promotional article in the *Encyclopaedia Britannica,* was built on the idea of self-preservation and preservation of the race. Whatever contributed to life was good; whatever shortened or detracted from life was evil. The article apparently assumed morality to be an evolutionary development, and with this I disagree. But what intrigued me was the article's insistence that preserving life was the very basis of morality.

In Christian terms, the morality of "choosing life" is heightened to the highest level because God commands it. Furthermore, choosing life means choosing eternal life.

To Choose Life Is a Moral Choice

To choose life by obeying the gospel is a moral decision because it is done in obedience to the will of God. Obedience to the gospel means to believe in the Lord Jesus Christ and be saved. To disobey the gospel will bring the wrath of God upon the disobedient (see Acts 16:31, Romans 1:5, 2 Thessalonians 1:8).

A change of mind toward God and faith in the Lord Jesus Christ (Acts 20:21) stems from a right perception of God and His righteousness. When the disciples of John repented of their sins and were baptized, they "justified God" (Luke 7:29, KJV). That is, they considered Him to be righteous in His character and in His judgment of sin. The change of mind and sorrow for sin which constitute repentance are in very essence moral. They form a moral victory for God.

To believe on the Lord Jesus Christ is to embrace "the way and the truth and the life" (John 14:6). To acknowledge that He is the only way to God is to declare God's righteousness. It is to affirm the very foundation of God's moral government of the universe. To receive Jesus as the truth is an exercise of faith's highest morality. As we have seen, to choose life is a moral choice, and to choose life that is the Life of God, holy and eternal, is to affirm His glory and to share it. And that is highly moral.

Man's Choice of God Glorifies God

The third question clamors to be answered: Would man's free choice of God and salvation add more to the glory and satisfaction of God than for Him to save us through sovereign, limited, and irresistible grace?

Our Lord Jesus Christ said the repentance of sinners brings joy in heaven. He repeats the statement twice, making it emphatic. The twice-repeated declaration of joy in heaven occurs in the parables of the lost sheep and the lost coin.

In the case of the lost sheep and the lost coin, the owners seek and find what was lost. Nothing is said about the attitude of the lost sheep, and, of course, the lost coin is incapable of any attitude at all. But, strangely enough, it is in connection with them that Jesus said repentance brings joy in heaven. Concerning the lost sheep, He said, "I tell you that in the same way there will be more rejoicing in heaven over one sinner who repents than over ninety-nine righteous persons who do not need to repent" (Luke 15:7). And in comparing the salvation of a repentant sinner to finding the lost coin, Jesus said, "In the same way, I tell you, there is rejoicing in the presence of the angels of God over one sinner who repents" (Luke 15:10).

Although the recovery of the sheep and the coin depended upon the activity of the owner, the joy in heaven wells up and overflows because sinners repent. Repentance is an affirmation of the righteousness and justice of God, the sinner's confession of his lack, and his appropriation of God's provision of righteousness in Christ. Repentance is a moral victory. It brings glory to God and joy in heaven.

The Prodigal Son Comes to Himself

A third parable in this passage in Luke concerns a lost son. Taking his inheritance from his father, he left home and set off for a distant country and there squandered his wealth in wild living. He plunged into the wilderness of unrestrained free moral choice and found it a moral jungle. Stripped of his fortune, his friends, and his honor, he ended up a swineherd, longing "to fill his stomach with the pods that the pigs were eating, but no one gave him anything" (Luke 15:16).

In this story, no one came to seek him, and there is no record of joy in heaven because of his repentance. The story tells what he did in the wilderness of free moral choice. It also makes clear that the memory of his father and the abundance of food in his household aroused him to arise and to go home.

The word "repentance" does not occur in the story of the prodigal, but its fact is clearly there. Nothing is said about the Son of Man who "came to seek and to save what was lost" (Luke 19:10). The prodigal is left in the jungle of free moral choice, where God is not overwhelmingly present in the brilliance of His glory.

Nevertheless, God *was* there working in the boy's heart through his empty stomach, and bringing about a change of mind by contrasting memories of his home with the hog pen of his circumstances. As a result, "he came to himself" (Luke 15:17, KJV; cf. 2 Chronicles 6:36-39). In response, the prodigal son uttered those memorable words of true repentance and moral resolve: "I will arise and go to my father, and will say unto him, Father I have sinned against heaven, and before thee. And am no more worthy to be called thy son; make me as one of thy hired servants." The sacred narrative goes on to say, "And he arose, and came to his father. But when he was yet a great way off, his father saw him, and had compassion, and ran, and fell on his neck, and kissed him" (Luke 15:18-20, KJV).

The prodigal's repentance and return brought feasting and joy in his father's house. It is a parable on earth portraying joy in heaven. Joy over repentance. The prodigal has chosen to come home.

God has permitted the human race to demand its inheritance and to turn the world into a moral wilderness. He has allowed man to come to a painful, experiential knowledge of good and evil and even to make choices with eternal consequences. God has made it clear, however, that it is His will that we choose life. He has no pleasure in the death of the wicked. He finds joy over repentant sinners.

Since God created mankind in His own image and likeness with the power of choice, I believe that more than anything else, God wanted man to love and to serve Him freely. It grieved God that man chose to believe and serve Satan and sin. But it delights His heart when man's darkened understanding is enlightened by the word and the Spirit so that he, with renewed perception, chooses to obey the gospel and to declare the righteousness of God.

Yes, man has been blinded by Satan and been taken captive, knows the passing pleasures of wild living, and "would long to fill his stomach with the pods the pigs were eating." But considering that God uses the helplessness of the captive and the hunger of the belly to show the folly of life apart from Him, and then grants a renewed vision of what is right, good, and expedient, is it not to the glory of God that man chooses to believe and ultimately to love Him? Does not this secure the kind of people and the kind of relationship God wants? Is it not a moral victory rather than simply an exercise of divine omnipotence?

"Adam, where are you?"

"God, where are You?"

In the wilderness of free moral agency, Satan is palpably present, God seemingly absent. But not really. For "from one man he made every nation of men, that they should inhabit the whole earth; and he determined the times set for them and the exact places where they should live. God did this so that men would seek him and perhaps reach out for him and find him, though he is not far from each one of us" (Acts 17:26-27).

Yes, man is free to choose, and that free choice, rightly made, glorifies God.

God's plan called for Him to share His sovereignty with His creatures, and in a very real—though limited—sense, He is captive to that choice. Men may freely choose what they will, sometimes despite God's stated desire.

For example, He wills all men to be saved and to come to the knowledge of the truth (1 Timothy 2:4), and is not willing that any should perish (2 Peter 3:9, Matthew 18:14). But we know that some will perish, by their own choice. Jesus lamented this tragic fact on the threshold of Jerusalem's destruction when He said of its people, "How often would I have gathered thy children together, even as a hen gathereth her chickens under her wings, and ye would not!" (Matthew 23:37, KJV).

Is this not another example of God Almighty delivering His might and glory into the hands of the enemy? God willed, men and women refused that will . . . and God permitted them their choice.

It seems utterly strange to us that God should be pleased to deliver His might and glory into His enemy's hand; and yet it is precisely there, though seemingly defeated and captive, that He quietly and powerfully works to free Satan's captives.

What about God's Choice?

In all this talk of choice, there is One whose freedom to choose has hardly been mentioned—God Himself. No one would deny that God makes absolutely free choices, yet this very ability raises a difficulty: If God has the freedom to choose whatever He wills, and if He has the power to accomplish those choices, then why does He not act to spare His children? Why does He allow the continued existence of evil?

We could spend a lifetime pondering that question and yet not fully grasp the answer, yet I still think it might be helpful to continue our inquiry there. Come with me as we plunge into that thorny question.

Chapter 5, Notes

1. Milton S. Terry, *Biblical Dogmatics* (n.p.: Eaton & Mains, 1907), p. 141.

CHAPTER 6

If God Is Able, Why Doesn't He Do Something about It?

THE question "why?" was removed from classroom complacency to disturbing concern for me one day when one of my male students at Multnomah School of the Bible was seized and forcibly raped while on his way to Sunday school.

For me, the question of why God allows bad things to happen to good people developed almost into a theological sickness. My mental anguish deepened when I heard one of God's choice servants tell of severe pain continuing at unbearable levels in spite of protracted prayer. She told of vacillating between "God is able to deliver" and "God is *not* able."

To the immediacy and nearness of this sort of evil, we can add the pain of uncounted millions in the blood-drenched pages of history and in contemporary disasters, persecutions, and genocides.

Who can measure the sufferings, feel the anguish, and bottle the tears of today's victims of war, famine, and oppression? And who is able to bring immediate comfort and lasting solution to their plight?

My wife and I are regular contributors to one or another Christian relief agency. At the same time, we have been keenly aware that God alone could adequately meet the need. "If God is able, why doesn't He act?"

In considering "why bad things happen to good people" and why the godly suffer, we dare not neglect the tragic fact that the good are often bad and the godly, even those called by His name, sometimes become ungodly in character and conduct.

Sin Is a Part of the Answer

The prophet Isaiah indicted his own people, Israel, with charges of iniquity so vile that though God was able to save, He refused to do so. Hear his words:

> Surely the arm of the LORD is not
>   too short to save,
>   nor his ear too dull to hear.
> But your iniquities have separated
>   you from your God;
> your sins have hidden his face from you,
>   so that he will not hear (Isaiah 59:1-2).

Such was the experience of Israel in the days of Samuel. The priesthood was corrupt, the people wicked. Consequently, the armies of Israel were defeated by their old enemies, the Philistines. The ark of God was taken and the glory of God departed from Israel.

Again and again God allowed His people to be subjugated by surrounding kings or be carried into captivity because of persistent sin. And He did so knowing that in their affliction, they would call upon Him.

The use of affliction to cause sinners to return to the Lord is the theme of Psalm 107. It is portrayed as a demonstration of the lovingkindness of God (vv. 1, 8-9, 15, 21, 31, 43).

The psalmist tells us that God afflicted the rebellious (v. 11), the fool (v. 17), and those who go down to the sea in ships (v. 23). In each case "they cried to the LORD in their trouble, and he saved them from their distress" (vv. 6, 13, 19, 28).

King David understood from experience God's use of affliction to restore his soul to right relation to God. He wrote, "I know, O LORD, that your laws are righteous, and in faithfulness you have afflicted me" (Psalm 119:75).

Similarly, the incestuous man at Corinth was delivered to Satan for the destruction of the flesh so that his spirit would be saved in the day of Christ.

A modern counterpart is found the current AIDS epidemic. The fear of AIDS has caused many in the homosexual community to consider the gospel, according to Richard Paradise, a pastor in the Sacramento area. As a result, a number have received Christ as their Savior. Recognizing that AIDS means an early appointment with death, they have turned to God in Christ to receive eternal life.

On the positive side, God has used affliction in the form of persecution, war, and natural disasters to turn the thoughts of uncounted thousands to God.

An article in the *Gospel Message* by Clifford Reimer and Abe Reddenkopp, titled "Ministering in a Hostile Environment," tells how God used persecution and violent opposition to build His church in Latin America:

> Opposition and violence have historically been the backdrop to rapid church growth. From 1949-1959, the period of *La Violencia* in Colombia, at least 300,000 people were killed—115 were evangelicals. Many church buildings were reduced to rubble. Christian schools were closed. Many believers—national and missionary—were jailed. The flip side is

God worked mightily, bringing many thousands to Himself. GMU [Gospel Missionary Union] churches doubled in the following decade.

Not surprisingly, in the current context of hostility, the number of conversions (3,600) in Colombia in 1987, was more than the total of all other GMU Latin American fields.

The radical growth of the evangelical church in Nicaragua during its recent history of incredible upheaval, caught many on-lookers off guard. Patrick Johnstone in his *Operation World* says, "The acute sufferings since 1977 due to war have made people seek after God . . . . Evangelicals have grown about 12% a year for the last 15 years, and are becoming a significant minority."

The working environment for missionaries is likely to become less safe as violence escalates. But history shows the church grows best in "wartime" not in "peacetime."[1]

When Bad Things Happen to Godly Saints

When the Philistines defeated Israel in two battles, killed thirty-four thousand soldiers, and captured the ark of God, the reasons for the debacle were clear.

God had warned that Hophni and Phinehas, the priests who carried the ark into the second battle, would die for their greed and moral corruption (1 Samuel 2:12-17, 22-36). Many others died because they were encouraged to sin by the example of these two wicked priests (1 Samuel 2:24).

But not all died because of their sin. As in the days of Elijah and the days of Paul, there was a godly remnant (Romans 11:1-5).

No doubt many went into battle pleading the promises of divine protection, counting upon the Lord to be their shield and defender. Others rested upon Israel's commission from God to exterminate the wicked nations in the Promised Land and to take it for their own possession. They remembered that in the past God had led Israel's armies in triumph over great kings and fortified cities. Many were sustained by a godly walk and unwavering faith.

But one thing happened to them all, to thirty-four thousand stout warriors—to the wicked, to the unbelieving, and to the devout.

They all died at the hand of their enemy.

Why were not the godly spared?

In previous chapters we considered the seeming absence of God in our hour of trial and temptation. How much easier it would be to make right choices if God hovered over us in a cherub-like helicopter with all lights flashing!

Up until now we pictured ourselves as originators of and participants in evil, and we wondered why God didn't intervene more openly to hinder us.

But now I want to consider a related but different theme. Here I envision us not so much as the authors of sin but as its victims, and suffering not because we made the wrong choices but because we made the right ones.

We have prayed, as instructed, "Deliver us from evil," and evil has befallen us. At least, so it appears to us. We say with Job, "When I hoped for good, evil came; when I looked for light, then came darkness" (Job 30:26). We seek to identify with the godly in Israel's army who perished at the hands of the Philistines.

Since God is all-loving, all-powerful, and all-wise, the persistence of evil touching the lives of those who have turned to God raises the cry, "Why doesn't He do something about it?"

The Example of Job

It is one thing to consider how God deals with those from whom He has hidden His face because of sin; it is another to contemplate God's seeming indifference to those whose saintliness marks them as God's chosen people. Of these, Job is the prototype of God's providential handiwork while Jesus is the antitype and the finished and perfected product. As the Captain of our salvation, Jesus was made perfect through suffering (Hebrews 2:10).

God selected Job out of his generation and out of all time to be subjected to unexplained suffering and humiliation at the hand of Satan (as a temptation to curse God rather than to continue to trust Him). He was chosen for this testing because God saw him as "blameless and upright, a man who fears God and shuns evil" (Job 1:8).

What followed took place not because Job had sinned and God was punishing him, but because Job was a God-fearing, good man. Satan contended that God bought off Job by prosperity, and if Job's wealth, health, and honor should be stripped from him, he would curse God to His face.

Thus the issue: Would man, created in the image of God as a free moral agent but corrupted by Adam's sin, choose to worship and serve God in spite of personal suffering and loss?

Satan said Job would curse God; God put Job in Satan's power.

This, however, was the climax, not the beginning of the contest between God and Satan over the faith of Job.

God Rated Job as Blameless and Upright

Before this fateful encounter, Job had reached a state of spiritual maturity which won for him the three-times-repeated evaluation: He was "blameless and upright, a man who feared God and shunned evil." And that was *God's* evaluation.

This must mean that there were earlier, ultimate, right choices made by Job arising out of his fear of God and hatred of evil. As a result, God prospered him, and now would test him.

I wish I knew the rules of the contest. It appears the goal of the game was to determine whom Job would believe and serve. I am reminded of that primal challenge given to Israel: "This day I call heaven and earth as witnesses against you that I have set before you life and death, blessings and curses. Now choose life, so that you and your children may live" (Deuteronomy 30:19).

It is hard to imagine how high the stakes were as God and Satan pitted themselves against each other for the choice Job would make. Doesn't this represent the ultimate "risk" that God took in granting free moral agency to His creatures? Satan had rebelled; Adam fell.

Would God pit His omniscience and omnipotence against Satan's perverted wisdom and persuasive, seductive beauty? While appearing to abandon Job, was God really (but secretly and infallibly) upholding him? Was Job after all but a pawn in the game between God and Satan? And was God somehow sustaining Job in his trials, though He ostensibly had abandoned him, and worse, was causing him to suffer for no good reason? Or could it be that God was available in response to Job's faith, though unseen and seemingly absent?

Whatever God may have been doing behind the scenes, Job didn't know about it and gained no comfort from it. Out of his agony, he complained:

> Even today my complaint is bitter;
> his hand is heavy in spite of my groaning.
> If only I knew where to find him;
> if only I could go to his dwelling!

. . . .

But if I go to the east, he is not there;
> if I go to the west, I do not find him
>> (Job 23:2-3, 8).

Tried Faith and Disappointed Love

Job's cry, "Though he slay me, yet will I hope in him," was wrung out of the testing and triumph of his faith. But the sob of the Shulammite in the Song of Solomon came from a deeply troubled heart as her love was tested and disappointed.

In the darkness of the night, her lover stood at her door seeking entrance. When she arose to let him in, he had disappeared. And she voiced the heartache of disappointed love:

My lover thrust his hand through the latch-opening;
> my heart began to pound for him.
I arose to open for my lover,
> and my hands dripped with myrrh,
my fingers with flowing myrrh,
> on the handles of the lock.
I opened for my lover,
> but my lover had left; he was gone.
> My heart sank at his departure.
I looked for him but did not find him.
> I called him but he did not answer
>> (Song of Solomon 5:4-6).

The Shulammite was denied the intimacy and anticipation of love and was left alone, abandoned.

She pictures well the anguish of a believer, also a lover of God, whose walk of warm intimacy with his Savior has been interrupted by some harshness of life in which God seems calloused and distant.

So it was with Mary and Martha when Lazarus was dying and Jesus purposely delayed His return to them.

In Romans chapter eight, those who love God and have been called according to His purpose mingle their groans with that of a creation in pain. But the sufferings of those who love God are more—not less—than the sufferings of creation. The lovers of God "face death all day long . . . are considered as sheep to be slaughtered" (Romans 8:36). It looks as if their Lover has abandoned them. Have you ever felt this way?

But love's confidence replies, "Who shall separate us from the love of Christ? . . . For I am convinced that neither death nor life, neither angels nor demons, neither the present nor the future, nor any powers, neither height nor depth, nor anything else in all creation, will be able to separate us from the love of God that is in Christ Jesus our Lord" (Romans 8:35, 38-39).

Agnes McDaniel, one-time dining hall supervisor and chief cook at Multnomah School of the Bible, saw death not as separating her from the love of God, but as bringing her home to the God she loved. She wrote joyously of this in a letter to family and friends dated August 27, 1988:

> Here I am today back in Portland, Oregon. I am traveling today on a new route, a new experience—the lovely (for me) Valley of the Shadow of Death. For some time I had been experiencing what I thought was my age and arthritis. However, my malady turns out to be cancer which is in my skull, my shoulders, my lungs, my bones, my hips and pelvis, and my leg. From the moment my doctor said this, I have been totally encompassed with God's loving care and so many experiences, that I could not write of so much. When he told me of the cancer's extent, I looked at him with eyes of delight and said robustly, "Doctor, you know what that means!" Through tears of joy, he

responded, "Yes, Agnes, because we know Him, it's *ultimate* healing."

All of you who know me know that for years I have talked openly and cheerfully of my great desire for heaven and home. To many I have said, "If you hear I died today, do not be sad, but go dance in the streets." We know that we cannot add a day or take one away—our times are appointed. But it appears that soon my redemption will be complete and I will see the great love of my soul—my Savior and my God.

Thus the saints who love God and the God who loves His own are held in love's embrace. Like Moses, we endure trials "as seeing him who is invisible" (Hebrews 11:27, KJV). With Peter, we love Him whom we have not seen (1 Peter 1:8). And though now we do not see Him—we fail to find Him in our distress—yet believing, we rejoice.

When Faith, Hope, and Love Are Disappointed, What Then?

If faith is disappointed, and love is disappointed, still we have hope. But if hope is deferred—if the answer does not come bringing relief from pain, deliverance from trial—then the heart is made sick (Proverbs 13:12).

How often have God's children felt like the man in the parable who went to his friend to ask for a loaf of bread at midnight to provide for unexpected guests. Has God seemed like the "friend" who replied, "Don't bother me. The door is already locked, and my children are with me in bed. I can't get up and give you anything" (Luke 11:7). But though God seems to be acting this way—doesn't want to be bothered, doesn't care about your plight—don't believe it. Keep on asking. "Put your hope in God" (Psalm 42:11).

Come with me to another bedside scene in a little home in Nova Scotia. Here hope found rest in firm faith. Six sons and daughters were gathered around their mother's bedside while two physicians ministered to her. For hours their patient had not moved or spoken, and finally every sign of life disappeared.

"She's gone," the doctors whispered.

But they spoke too soon.

That stout-hearted mother had one more work of faith to do. Sitting up in bed, she rallied her strength and prayed in a clear tone, "Lord, I thank Thee . . . once more . . . for putting my Bernard into the gospel ministry."

At that time, Bernard B. Sutcliffe, her seventh child, was far from the scene of his mother's deathbed and farther still from faith in his mother's God.

Assured that God had heard her prayer of faith for her son's salvation and for his usefulness in the gospel ministry, Mrs. Sutcliffe settled back upon her pillow and the Lord took her home.

Three years later this mother's wayward son came to know Christ as Savior.

Following his conversion, B. B. Sutcliffe became bold in his testimony and diligent in Bible study. He served on the faculty and extension staff of Moody Bible Institute, on the faculty of Dallas Seminary, and became a co-founder and the first president of Multnomah School of the Bible.

He became a great Bible expositor and a devoted man of God. But it was his godly mother whose faith claimed his salvation and service for God. She did not believe that the gospel's picture of a man in bed with his children was intended to represent God as reluctant to answer prayer. Rather, she believed what Jesus said: "Ask, and it will be given to you; seek, and you will find; knock, and it will be opened to you" (Luke 11:9, NKJV).

Resilient Faith

Some of the Jews who faced death in the Holocaust might well be added to the faith heroes of Hebrews 11.

Like the early Christian martyrs, these Jews were mocked, tortured, and put to death. And although God did not answer their prayers for here-and-now deliverance, they sang of their faith in Him:

I really do believe that the Messiah is coming very soon.

And even though You are not here,
We are waiting for You.
We are worshiping You.
Heavenly Father, we trust in You.

Job's faith, the Shulammite's love, and the hopes of many of God's choice people have sought for God in desperate hours—and did not find Him. Like the Shulammite, Faith, Love, and Hope could say, "I looked for him but did not find him. I called him but he did not answer."

Nevertheless, Faith, Love, and Hope, like Job, have not been in complete darkness. They share something of Job's perception that God was testing him and would find him faithful. Let us allow Job to speak of his faith in God and of his confidence that his testing would do him good:

But he knows the way that I take;
when he has tested me, I will come forth as gold.
My feet have closely followed his steps;
I have kept to his way without turning aside.
I have not departed from the commands of his lips;
I have treasured the words of his mouth
more than my daily bread (Job 23:10-12).

Job's confidence that he would emerge from the fires of trial as refined gold finds echoes in the writing of the apostle Peter. He would encourage us that trials "have come so that your faith—of greater worth than gold, which perishes even though refined by fire—may be proved genuine and may result in praise, glory and honor when Jesus Christ is revealed" (1 Peter 1:7).

And again, "Dear friends, do not be surprised at the painful trial you are suffering, as though something strange were happening to you. But rejoice that you participate in the sufferings of Christ, so that you may be overjoyed when his glory is revealed" (1 Peter 4:12-13).

Bad things may happen to God's good people to test their faith, to refine and develop their character, and to enable them to see the hand of the invisible God working all things together for good in their lives—that is, their eternal good.

Why must God's people "face death all day long" and be "considered as sheep to be slaughtered"?

Why are the faith, love, and hope of God's people subjected to trial and disappointment?

In the next chapter we shall see that the self-limited God is still able to do immeasurably more than all we ask or imagine . . . and that He is going to do it. But all too often what He is doing may not be known until we get to heaven.

Chapter 6, Notes

1. Clifford Reimer and Abe Reddenkopp, "Ministering in a Hostile Environment," *Gospel Message*, vol. 97, no. 1 (1989), p. 5.

CHAPTER 7

God Is Able and He Is Working

THERE is bitter irony in the story of John the Baptist.

As the forerunner of the Messiah, John preached in the wilderness of Judea, saying, "Repent, for the kingdom of heaven is near" (Matthew 3:2). "People went out to him from Jerusalem and all Judea and the whole region of the Jordan. Confessing their sins, they were baptized by him in the Jordan River" (Matthew 3:5-6).

John was "great in the sight of the Lord" and "filled with the Holy Spirit" (Luke 1:15). He rebuked the religious leaders as a "brood of vipers" and called tax gatherers and soldiers to repentance and honesty. He was the forerunner of the King, preaching God's kingdom message "in the spirit and power of Elijah" (Luke 1:17).

And yet he ended up in prison for charging Herod with unlawful marriage to his brother's wife—imprisoned, not because of evil, but because he did what God told him to do.

Apparently no one told John why his King would not break him out of jail. Why would this Jesus do nothing? Was He really the King?

John sent some of his disciples to Jesus to find out. Was Jesus the Promised One, or should they look for another? Jesus told John's messengers, "Go back and report to John what you hear and see: The blind receive sight, the lame walk, those who have leprosy are cured, the deaf hear, the dead are raised, and the good news is preached to the poor. Blessed is the man who does not fall away on account of me" (Matthew 11:4-6).

Then Jesus eulogized John, applying the words of Isaiah to him: "I will send my messenger ahead of you, who will prepare your way before you" (Matthew 11:10).

Did this preparation include the repentant in Israel? Did John's martyrdom prepare Jesus for His own crucifixion? Did not Jesus depart alone to a desert place when He heard of John's death?

Before Herod sent for the head of John and presented it on a platter to the daughter of Herodias, was that head plagued with doubts and fears? "If God is able, why doesn't He deliver me? If the kingdom is at hand, why am I left in prison?"

And why did God's script for John and for Jesus include ironic mockery of triumphant power and popularity, followed by ignominious death?

We do not know how much John the Baptist knew about affliction working eternal reward for the godly. Nor do we know how much this precious truth sustained him in his worst hours. But he knows it now.

Temporary Suffering, Eternal Glory

So does the apostle Paul. John and Paul have entered into the joy of their Lord. They have heard Him say, "Well done!"

What the apostle experienced about suffering and rewards he recorded in 2 Corinthians 4:17-18: "For our light and momentary troubles are achieving for us an eternal glory that far outweighs them all. So we fix our eyes not on what is seen, but on what is unseen. For what is seen is temporary, but what is unseen is eternal."

In Hebrews 11 we are told that faith is being sure of what we hope for and having a conviction concerning what we do not see. The word "conviction" strongly suggests the work of the Holy Spirit in bringing to light and understanding the invisible things of God. Thus Moses forsook Egypt, not fearing the wrath of Pharaoh, "because he saw him who is invisible" (Hebrews 11:27).

Yet Moses and Israel in those early years of their history saw more of the presence and power of God displayed on their behalf than any other nation or people in any other time. The absence of the miraculous displays of God's providential care in Israel's later history caused Gideon to cry out for his forsaken people. He said:

> If the LORD is with us, why has all this happened to us? Where are all his wonders that our fathers told us about when they said, "Did not the LORD bring us up out of Egypt?" But now the LORD has abandoned us and put us into the hand of Midian (Judges 6:13).

Back in Hebrews, note the change in God's dealings with His people, especially those selected for inclusion with the great heroes of faith. When time failed the author to note the exploits of more faith heroes, he summarized the kinds of victories they achieved: They "conquered kingdoms, administered justice, and gained what was promised; who shut the mouths of lions, quenched the fury of the flames, and escaped the edge of the sword; whose weakness was turned to strength; and who became powerful in battle and routed foreign armies. Women received back their dead, raised to life again."

Then comes the change: "Others were tortured and refused to be released, so that they might gain a better resurrection. Some faced jeers and flogging, while still others were chained and put in prison. They were stoned; they were sawed in two; they were put to death by the sword. They went about in sheepskins and goatskins, destitute, persecuted and mistreated" (Hebrews 11:33-37).

These latter faith heroes were not junior grade, second class. They were not rejects whose faltering prayers failed to reach the ear of God. On the contrary, "the world was not worthy of them" (Hebrews 11:38).

They were the superconquerors who had endured tribulation, distress, persecution, famine, nakedness, peril, and sword. Of them Paul wrote, "As it is written: 'For your sake we face death all day long; we are considered as sheep to be slaughtered.' No, in all these things we are more than conquerors through him who loved us" (Romans 8:36-37).

In their sufferings, God's providence met His predestination. They, and we, are predestined to be conformed to the image of His Son. And providential sufferings form a part of the transforming process.

The Mind of Christ as a Lifestyle

To be conformed to the image of Christ includes the transformation of our minds. To have the "mind of Christ" does not mean benign, arm's-length approval of Christ's self-emptying and obedience unto death, but rather a life shaped by the stern reality of self-sacrifice: ". . . if indeed we share in his sufferings in order that we may also share in his glory" (Romans 8:17).

To accept the martyr as a superconqueror requires a mindset unlike that of the world and like that of Christ. Along with the world, we are prone to acclaim as victorious the army that crushes and destroys. The song of Moses celebrated such victory as the nation of Israel exulted over its enemies who had drowned in the Red Sea. Yes, *exulting* over literal, dead enemies.

Doesn't your heart respond to this excerpt from that song of victory?

I will sing to the LORD,
>   for he is highly exalted.
The horse and its rider
>   he has hurled into the sea.

. . . .

Your right hand, O LORD
>   was majestic in power.
Your right hand, O LORD,
>   shattered the enemy.
In the greatness of your majesty
>   you threw down those who opposed you.
You unleashed your burning anger;
>   it consumed them like stubble (Exodus 15:1, 6-7).

We would find it easy to replace the armies of Pharaoh with some modern enemy and rejoice in his utter defeat. What about terrorists who bomb public places or hijackers who kill innocent passengers?

If God is able, why doesn't He act?

The Song and the Way of the Lamb

Why doesn't God intervene if He is able? It's because there is another song. It is called the song of the Lamb—the Lamb that was slain, the "Lamb of God who takes away the sin of the world."

And they sang a new song:

>   You are worthy . . . because you were slain,
>>   and with your blood you purchased
>>   men for God
>>   from every tribe and language and
>>   people and nation. . . .
>   Worthy is the Lamb, who was slain,
>>   to receive power and wealth and
>>   wisdom and strength
>   and honor and glory and praise!
>   (Revelation 5:9, 12).

The song of the Lamb celebrates the victory of the cross. He was "crucified through weakness," yet plundered principalities and powers, triumphing over them (2 Corinthians 13:4, Colossians 2:15, KJV). He took on flesh and blood so that "by his death he might destroy him who holds the power of death—that is, the devil" (Hebrews 2:14). "Christ died for our sins" (1 Corinthians 15:3).

The cross sheds light upon our question, "If God is able, why doesn't He act—our way?" Why doesn't He allow us to sing the song of Moses? Because for now, there is another song—and the way—of the Lamb.

And yet, in His footsteps and by His power we can be more than conquerors—or literally, superconquerors—in all these things which are against us.

Note that the persecuting enemy continues in strength and control, whether enemy government or unrelieved pain. But the power of God gives grace, endurance, and testimony "in all these things"—not in getting out of them, or in conquering or vanquishing as the world counts victory, but "in" them.

Well do I remember seeking to comfort an elderly woman, dying of cancer but living in Christ. I started to say, "We can't understand why God permits . . . "

She interrupted: "We don't need to understand. It is enough that God permits it."

Her afflictions—seen as both light and momentary—have worked for her a great and eternal glory that far outweighs them all.

Paul's letter to the Colossians lists several prayer concerns. He prayed that they would know the will of God, walk worthily of the Lord, be fruitful in good works, increase in the knowledge of God, and be strengthened by the power of God (Colossians 1:9-11).

If our hearts are set upon singing the song of Moses—the song of the God who is able to act, and does it now—we will be disappointed. Like Naaman, the Old

Testament leper, we'd prefer a full-blown, multi-colored, Fourth-of-July-style miracle.

But no. Not lion-like power but Lamb-like submission.

Paul prayed that they (and we!) would be "strengthened with all might, according to his glorious power, unto all patience and longsuffering with joyfulness" (Colossians 1:11, KJV).

What a letdown! If strengthened with "all power," why can't we flex our spiritual muscles? Why don't we solve some unsolvable problem, beat down some mighty enemy, charge ahead invincibly with the unmistakable power of God? Why not make bread of some stones?

God's Rock-Polishing Machine

Maybe we could we put it this way. Suppose all the hydroelectric power from all the dams on the Columbia River was channeled into one massive power line. Imagine that instead of lighting and heating cities and running the wheels of vast industries, it was attached to a single rock-polishing machine. Incongruous! The power would be totally out of proportion to the job.

In the same way, it seems to us that omnipotence is not given a chance to flex its muscles when limited to producing in us patience and long-suffering with joyfulness. But "seems" is an important word; for it is much harder to build character than to create a world.

Could it be that we have underestimated the challenge to God's omnipotence? Remember that omnipotence is captive to a plan in which the public miracle, the irrefutable demonstration of divine power, is not the order of the day (or age).

Consequently, God's omnipotence is not normally destroying His enemies and rescuing His people in miraculous displays of power. God is rather strengthening the inner man in order that we may endure the hardships of life and say with Job, "though he slay me, yet will

I hope in him." And that is indeed a job fit for omnipotence! Especially to make us do it with joyfulness!

The sufferings of Christ which bore in our place the penalty of sin were finished on the cross—never to be repeated.

But the sufferings of the body of Christ—that mystical organism composed of all true believers in this age—are not yet complete.

We Fill Up the Sufferings of the Body of Christ

The apostle Paul wrote that his own sufferings helped to fill up the sufferings of the body of Christ (Colossians 1:24). Peter also refers to our becoming partakers of Christ's sufferings (1 Peter 4:13).

A story from *National Review* illustrates what they mean.

Some years ago a right-wing coup d'état overturned the leftist government of Chile. A female doctor ministered to the wounded from armies of both factions and was soon thrown in prison. There she was raped by one of her guards.

This woman possessed unusual spiritual discernment, and according to her own account of her terrifying and shameful experience, her thoughts were filled with the idea that she was filling up the sufferings of the body of Christ. This mystic awareness overshadowed the normal indignation which such an experience brings.

The fact that God has allowed His people to be thus debased has always been a problem for me. To allow martyrdom, yes—but why, O Lord, do You not bare your omnipotent arm and strike down the rapist who lays filthy hands upon godly women who have entrusted their virtue to You? That has been hard for me to accept. The experience of the Chilean has helped.

Yes, Christ was made sin for us, including all the ugly sins. Filling up the sufferings of the body of Christ has included them, too. Today I understand better how omnipotence is needed to produce in us patience and long-suffering with joyfulness.

The Wheat and the Tares Are to Grow Together

It is important to remember that God, captive to His own plan, has determined to let the wheat and tares grow together until the harvest. Like the landowner who instructed his servants not to pull out the tares in his field, so God allows wicked men to grow and flourish alongside His own people. He is long-suffering, not now imputing trespasses (2 Peter 3:9, 2 Corinthians 5:19, KJV).

Both the tares and the wheat will grow to maturity, and in their maturation fully display their essential character. Then comes judgment!

If humanitarian love and pity for a helpless victim join with moral indignation to make us want to destroy the destroyer, how much more must love and holiness in God move Him to avenge His own and to deliver them?

How often, then, must God have restrained His anger against the wicked and have shared the sorrows of the oppressed rather than bringing immediate relief?

When the Lord saw how great was the wickedness of men in the days of Noah, "The LORD was grieved that he had made man on the earth, and his heart was filled with pain" (Genesis 6:6). And in the days of Hosea, God's heart broke as He found it necessary to judge Israel. The prophet recorded the heartache of God:

> How can I give you up, Ephraim?
>> How can I hand you over, Israel?
> How can I treat you like Admah?
>> How can I make you like Zeboiim?
> My heart is changed within me;
>> all my compassion is aroused (Hosea 11:8).

When we give our little to bring relief from famine and God seems to do nothing at all directly—when He could easily remedy the whole problem—He must indeed suffer as He witnesses the agony and deaths of millions of people. He is a God of love and compassion, touched with the feeling of our infirmities. And "in all their afflictions he was afflicted." How easy and how natural it would be for Him to wipe away every tear, to blot out every sorrow, and to replace pain with pleasure!

God Uses Affliction to Get Our Attention

A part of the reason God does not do what His love and pity long to do is that He must get man's attention and humble his pride. God resists the proud and gives grace to the humble (James 4:6, KJV). And He resists and humbles the proud in order to call attention to His grace.

You probably have heard the story of a man who sold a mule with every assurance to the buyer that the mule was well trained and would obediently respond to bit, bridle, and spoken word.

The buyer hitched up his new purchase only to find it wholly unresponsive. He went to the seller, complained, and brought him back to see what was wrong.

Without a word the mule's former owner picked up a two-by-four and hit the mule square on the head. "You've got to get his attention first," he said.

God used even more drastic measures than this to get the attention of His headstrong and unrepentant people. The psalmist recounts that "when He killed them, then they sought Him" (Psalm 78:34, NASB). So it was when God sent the fiery serpents among His complaining people. Hosea notes the principle involved: "In their misery they will earnestly seek me" (Hosea 5:15).

God's providential judgments are clothed in mercy. Could it have been that many who perished in the flood found eternal life because in their death they called upon the Lord?

Missionaries from famine-plagued lands report that God has used famine to capture the attention of the indifferent and to humble the proud, all so that they might consider the grace of God in Christ. Yes, God uses affliction to cause people to turn to Him.

God's Tough Love Calls for Perfection

The quality of God's love has in recent days acquired a new, descriptive adjective: tough love. It is opposed to soft and sentimental love, indulgent and protective. It is tough because it moves us toward conformity to Jesus Christ. It is not content to let us admire Christ; we must acquire Him—the mind of Christ, the power of His resurrection, the fellowship of His sufferings. We must be made perfect, like the Captain of our salvation, through suffering.

"Because You love me," we plead, "take the heat off of me. Leave me alone!"

But because He loves, He chastens us that we may be partakers of His holiness (Hebrews 12:10, 1 John 3:1-2).

In our age we must learn the song of the Lamb, and be led as sheep to the slaughter, to demonstrate to principalities and powers that love is stronger than hate, that sacrifice, both *His* and *ours*, is the stuff out of which eternal salvation is made.

God is bound by His tough love not to do all that His power would allow Him to do, because He wants to bring us through testing to triumph, through suffering to glory, and by following the Captain of our salvation to be made like Him.

CHAPTER 8

We Are Able, Why Don't We Act?

I have dared to ask, "If God is able, why doesn't He act?"

But how will you answer His question, "If you are able, why don't *you* act?"

All of us will answer that question at the judgment seat of Christ. Then we will receive the things done in the body, whether good or bad (2 Corinthians 5:10).

Because God works *in* us what we are to work *out*, "we are able"—able by the grace of God—to labor abundantly, effectively, and not in vain.

As Paul puts it in 1 Corinthians 15, our labor is not in vain in the Lord, because God's grace in our lives is not in vain, and because our faith in the resurrected Savior is not in vain (vv. 2, 10, 14, 17, 58).

> Therefore, my dear brothers, stand firm. Let nothing move you. Always give yourselves fully to the work of the Lord, because you know that your labor in the Lord is not in vain (1 Corinthians 15:58).

The Scriptures recount the exploits of men and women empowered by the Spirit of God. They remind us that God can take ordinary people and enable them to do great things for the kingdom. "We are able" because "He is able"—"able to do immeasurably more than all we ask or imagine, according to his power that is at work within us" (Ephesians 3:20). As we meditate upon verses like these, may we say with the apostle Paul, "Lord, what will You have me to do?"

We do not have to go back to Hebrews 11 to find giants of faith. We have them today. They endure persecution. They say, "We ought to obey God rather than men." In the face of hate, they say, "I love you."

They serve humbly in obscurity, finding greatness in servanthood.

They serve brilliantly, boldly, and successfully.

They have forsaken all and followed Jesus.

By birth, they are large or small, strong or weak, bold or timid, talented or limited, but by the grace of God, they are able—able to do exploits for God.

They sacrifice heroically. Some give the widow's mite, others more easily give millions. They have brought relief to thousands who otherwise would have perished through war, famine, and disease. In the language of Hebrews 11, time and space would fail me to tell of all the modern faith heroes through whom God has done great things.

We could mention Billy Graham and Luis Palau among the evangelists touching millions for Christ through campaigns, radio, television, and books and magazines.

Ken Taylor comes to mind as the paraphraser of *The Living Bible* and head of a great publishing firm.

Consider Bill Bright. He founded Campus Crusade for Christ in 1951, and currently has some sixteen thousand full-time and associate staff members ministering in more than 150 countries. His vision has resulted in training millions in practical and fruitful methods of introducing people to Christ. Uncounted numbers have come to saving faith. Current training plans envision vastly expanded ministry through video and films.

Bill was one of many promising young people whom Henrietta Mears of Hollywood Presbyterian Church instructed and inspired and sent on their way to do great things for God.

Then recall the vision and exploits of Cameron Townsend and his Wycliffe Bible Translators. He and they have translated the word of God into thousands of languages and opened the door of salvation to tribes and peoples who would otherwise never know God's word and way of salvation. Thousands of choice men and women have responded to the call to become translators and have forsaken the comforts and luxuries of home to live and serve among primitive peoples and savage cultures.

We cannot begin to do justice to the great impact of all the evangelical Bible colleges, Christian liberal arts colleges, and graduate schools of theology. But let me mention two.

Dallas Seminary materialized from the vision of Dr. Lewis Sperry Chafer. A recent letter from President Donald K. Campbell summarizes something of the strategic places of leadership occupied by the school's alumni:

> Today the presidents of 45 Bible schools, colleges, and seminaries are Dallas graduates. More than 400 DTS alumni serve as missionaries in 70 countries. And more than 1,494 senior pastors and 492 associate pastors in America today are DTS alumni.

And while we are thinking about the influence of schools, let me tell you about Multnomah School of the Bible, founded in 1936. God gave a vision to Dr. John G.

Mitchell for a Bible school in the Northwest, and he shared that vision with Dr. B. B. Sutcliffe, Rev. Simon E. Forsberg, and me—all of whom became co-founders of the school along with several businessmen.

As of August 1989, Multnomah claims 11,537 alumni, of whom more than 970 have served as missionaries at home and abroad. The pastorate has attracted some 483 alumni. Youth pastors number 47. Other Christian organizations list 215 alumni as staff members. Thousands bear their witness in industry, business and professional vocations, and as homemakers. What a force for God and for good!

Bert and Colleen Elliot, Multnomah alumni, recently were honored by the Brethren Assemblies along the Amazon River in Peru. In the forty years they have served as pioneer missionaries, they have established some fifty churches. In recognition of their service to the people of the province of Cajamarca, the civil government presented Bert an award and an honorary doctor's degree.

Not only have evangelists, prominent pastors, radio and television preachers, and college and seminary leaders been inspired and empowered by God to do prodigious works, but many less known are serving Him faithfully and fruitfully in places of humble yet strategic service.

There was a Mr. Wright who spent hours a day in his basement, seated by his furnace, bringing names and needs to God's attention from his long prayer list.

Many will remember R. G. LeTourneau, maker of heavy earth-moving equipment and founder of LeTourneau College. His giving reversed the ancient tithe of Mosaic law. He kept the tithe and gave 90 percent to God.

You, no doubt, could add many names to these heroes of the faith. Some are known only to yourself, others stand in the limelight because of well-known accomplishments.

Yes, we by grace are able, and many are doing great things for God.

The Holy Spirit Empowers

The record of the working of the Holy Spirit in the early church makes it clear that the Spirit empowered believers to work miracles, to overcome satanic opposition, and to witness effectively. "Being filled with the Spirit" is how the early church was made strong to do the will of God. We are commanded to be filled in Ephesians 5:18.

To be filled with the Spirit is the believer's responsibility. This involves hungering and thirsting after God. It means inviting Jesus Christ to reign in your heart. It calls for a daily walk in dependence upon the Spirit's delivering power.

But we do not always meet these conditions. Ananias and Sapphira didn't (see Acts 5). Rather, they lied to the Holy Spirit by pretending to make a greater sacrificial gift to the welfare of the church than they actually gave. Others grieve the Holy Spirit by unconfessed sin. Still others limit His working through their unbelief.

God's Work Is Often Captive to the Church

If the union of God and man formed in the womb of Mary meant limitation and humbling for God incarnate, how much greater the limitation and humbling must be for God to indwell redeemed-yet-sinful human hearts! Could God shrink from that association, as did the apostle Paul when he realized his sinful corruption and cried out, "What a wretched man I am! Who will rescue me from this body of death?" (Romans 7:24).

Paul's cry may have reflected a cruel and ghastly form of death penalty. In it a dead body was tied to a living one: face to face, mouth to mouth, hands to hands, until the death from the dead invaded and claimed the living.[1]

How often have we, like Paul, cried out for deliverance from our wretched wickedness? Our sins distress us even though we realize that they have been forgiven.

If we are disgraced by our sinful nature and sinful conduct, how much more must the indwelling Christ be shamed? If our unfruitfulness prompts men to "gather and burn" us (John 15:6), how can Christ be unburned?

Recently a popular newspaper column scorched a radio preacher for his unethical methods of fund-raising. The column blazed with righteous indignation, flamed with telling sarcasm, and consumed the evangelist's professed integrity as though it were wood, hay, and stubble. I laughed aloud and felt the article expressed my own feelings. I shared it (and my own "righteous indignation") with others.

And then I remembered that Christ was also burned in the fire.

How tragic that so many who identify with God's cause—thus making Him captive to their reputations—have been selfish, carnal, dishonest, and disgraceful. Was not the name of God blasphemed because of Israel's unfaithfulness (Romans 2:24)? And who among us has not brought dishonor upon the name of God because of willful sin? How often unbelievers have said, "If that is Christianity, I don't want it." May God enable us to live as we ought!

Captive to Our Cooperation

What parent has not felt that it would be easier to get a job done if he did it himself, rather than asking his child to do it? I wonder if God doesn't sometimes feel that way about us. If God could speak creation into being, and if Jesus could have summoned twelve legions of angels to do His bidding, why does God choose to become captive to our cooperation? And yet that is exactly what He does.

If getting things done in heaven and on earth depended solely upon the exercise of God's omnipotence, then there would be no need for us to pray, "Your will be done on earth as it is in heaven" (Matthew 6:10). The prayer implies that God's perfect will for this earth is being opposed and that God is counting upon our prayers to help. We are to go into all the world and to teach all nations (Matthew 28:19).

The Bible is plain that God does not do some things He would like to do, simply because we have not prayed for them: "You do not have, because you do not ask God," James says. "Pray for us that the message of the Lord may spread rapidly and be honored," writes Paul. "The harvest is plentiful but the workers are few. Ask the Lord of the harvest, therefore, to send out workers into his harvest field," said Jesus. The results belong to God. But He expects our cooperation.

God requires that our salvation be "worked out" in life. He forms a partnership with us, enabling us to work out in practical service His inwrought salvation. That is the message of Philippians 2:12-13: "Wherefore, my beloved, as ye have always obeyed, not as in my presence only, but now much more in my absence, work out your own salvation with fear and trembling. For it is God which worketh in you both to will and to do of his good pleasure" (KJV).

So far, so good. But if it is true that God works in the believer "both to will and to do according to his good pleasure," might we not expect better results?

One young pastor was jolted into that realization one Sunday after the close of the morning service. He stood at the door of his church greeting his people as they left. Many thanked him for his sermon, and each time he modestly deferred to the Lord as the source of any blessing. He expected another such exchange when a familiar face approached.

"Thank you, pastor, for a good message this morning," a pleasant woman said.

"Don't thank me. Thank the Lord," the pastor replied.

"Oh, it wasn't that good," the woman declared.

Somehow, even when we work out our sermons with fear and trembling, God is plainly captive to our limitations.

The Danger of Limiting God

This captivity could well extend to our theologies. Could it be that there are doctrinal claims and counterclaims which limit and frustrate the saving work of God?

And what of our methods of bringing Christ to a lost world? Are we substituting "come to church" for "go into all the world"? Is God longing to break out of the captivity of our stained glass windows to reach out to a world dying in the inner city, dying in the streets, dying in jails and hospitals?

Our failure to work out our own salvation can do nothing but hinder the grace of God—hence His exhortation to get busy at it.

When Jesus visited His own hometown, "he did not do many miracles there because of their lack of faith" (Matthew 13:58). Lack of faith ties God's hands and thwarts the desires of His compassionate heart. How can we respond to our duty to pray in any other way than to ask, as did His disciples, "Lord, teach us to pray"? And to plead, in the words of the distraught father on behalf of his son, "Lord, I believe; help my unbelief!"

Since the body of Christ is made up of all kinds of believers, some weak and some strong, some selfish and others self-sacrificing, God reaches out to a lost world through hands too often grasping for personal gain and feet running after pleasure. Do we imprison Him in our own selfishness? Do we shame Him, like Samson, by living self-indulgent and impure lives?

But I have dwelt long enough on the negative. There is a glorious, positive side to the realized potential of the members of the body of Christ. By the grace of God, men and women, boys and girls, have done exploits in Christ's name. They have turned the world—and its values!—upside down.

The Early Church Was Able

James and John said, "We can," in answering Jesus' question, "Can you drink the cup I am going to drink?" (Matthew 20:22).

Peter also proclaimed his ability to stand loyal to Christ: "Lord, I am ready to go with you to prison and to death" (Luke 22:33). Though all men should betray Him, Peter said he would stand true.

But it didn't work out that way—until Pentecost. Then there descended upon the apostles and disciples the enabling power of the Holy Spirit; and in His power, heroes of the faith have been empowered to say, "We are able."

Anticipating the formation of the "body of Christ" on the day of Pentecost, Jesus said, "But you will receive power when the Holy Spirit comes on you . . ." (Acts 1:8).

The employment of that power, however, was conditional. It depended first upon faith in the Lord Jesus Christ who said concerning the Holy Spirit, "Whoever believes in me, as the Scripture has said, streams of living water will flow from within him" (John 7:38). Those who repented of crucifying Christ were baptized in His name and received the gift of the Holy Spirit (Acts 2:38).

Following Pentecost, the infant church was threatened and persecuted by the leaders of Israel. In response, the church prayed to God for boldness to speak His word, and "they were all filled with the Holy Spirit and spoke the word of God boldly" (Acts 4:31).

Because of Pentecost, We Are Able

The church of Jesus Christ is God's special agent. He works through us. We are His servants, His witnesses, His ambassadors, and workers together with God. We are His feet to run with the news of salvation, His hands to work until night comes. In the amazing words of Ephesians 1:23, we are "his body, the fulness of him that filleth all in all" (KJV). He is bound to us, captive to His body, in accomplishing His work in the world. We are now able to drink His cup, to suffer and to die as His witnesses.

Sometimes we mistakenly think that our personal inadequacies or family shortcomings or underprivileged backgrounds keep us from doing what God has called us to do. We think we're too weak or too uneducated or too old or too young or too busy or too tired or too poor or too you-name-it. We need to consider the words of Tim Hansel in his marvelous book, *You Gotta Keep Dancin'*:

> Most of the Psalms were born in difficulty. Most of the Epistles were written in prisons. Most of the greatest thoughts of the greatest thinkers of all time had to pass through the fire. Bunyan wrote *Pilgrim's Progress* from jail. Florence Nightingale, too ill to move from her bed, reorganized the hospitals of England. Semiparalyzed and under the constant menace of apoplexy, Pasteur was tireless in his attack on disease. During the greater part of his life, American historian Francis Parkman suffered so acutely that he could not work for more than five minutes at a time. His eyesight was so wretched that he could scrawl only a few gigantic words on a manuscript, yet he contrived to write twenty magnificent volumes of history. Sometimes it seems that when God is about to make preeminent use of a man, he puts him through the fire.[2]

And Tim Hansel models his message. Living in near constant pain, he keeps on "dancing" and leading others into a life of joy in the Lord. We, too, can be "more than conquerors." We are

- able to live pleasing to God in progressive holiness.

- able to care for the helpless, the hungry, and the dying.

- able to witness effectively to God's saving grace in Christ.

"Not that we are competent in ourselves to claim anything for ourselves, but our competence comes from God" (2 Corinthians 3:5). We are workers together with God (2 Corinthians 6:1). It is like the teamwork I witnessed of two Nicaraguans sawing out lumber with a dragsaw. As I remember the scene, a log was lying on a raised platform. One worker stood above the log and the other beneath it. Together they pulled and pushed the sharp saw through the log to cut dimension lumber.

Yes, in Christ, *we are able.*

But not all of us fall into the noble train of faith heroes. Not all realize that we are able and do something about it. Why don't we? Why don't you? Why don't I?

How are we responding to the unlimited possibilities of faith in the greatness of God? What have we done with Jesus' invitation to do the miraculous? Have we commanded mountains to move? Hear once more His challenge to do wonders:

> . . . if you have faith as small as a mustard seed,
> you can say to this mountain, "Move from here
> to there" and it will move. Nothing will be
> impossible for you (Matthew 17:20).

If we have stopped short of mountain-moving faith, have we tried a lesser miracle—that of commanding the mulberry tree to be uprooted and planted in the sea (Luke 17:6)? Or have we taught others the potential of faith while never really trying it ourselves?

My good friend, Carl E. Anderson, now with his Lord, rose to the challenge of faith and proved God faithful time and again.

He began his training for the ministry at Moody Bible Institute. Since he did not enjoy robust health, he determined to devote his limited energies to study. He would trust God for his material needs. Even when school bills pressed heavily upon him and school authorities advised him to get a job or to drop out, he resolutely persisted in trusting God. Why preach that God will supply all your needs if you have not experienced it in your own life?

God did not test him above what he was able to bear. His testing ended at a Moody missionary conference. He stood to his feet in response to a call to give his life for missionary service. A godly woman in the audience, a Mrs. Gibson of the Gibson greeting card family, saw him volunteer, inquired about his need, and paid for his schooling throughout Moody Bible Institute, Wheaton College, and Dallas Seminary. Not a mountain of impossibility, perhaps, but a tough-rooted mulberry tree was plucked up and cast into the sea!

The haunting question "Why don't we?" appears again in the following parable:

> I arrived early one morning. It was cold; there were flurries of snow on the ground, and I noticed that while the service attendants and skycaps were warmly dressed in heavy coats and gloves, oddly enough, they wore no shoes. I hustled inside and soon saw that no one there wore shoes, either. I went to baggage claim, picked up my luggage, and boarded a shuttle to my hotel. None of my fellow travelers wore

shoes. When we arrived at the hotel, I found the bellhop, the clerk, and everyone else all barefoot.

I asked the manager what this practice meant. "What practice?" he said. "Why," I replied, pointing to his bare feet, "why don't you wear shoes in this town?" "Ah," he said, "that is just it. Why don't we?" "But why? Don't you believe in shoes?" "Believe in shoes, my friend? I should say we do. We believe in shoes more than anything. They are indispensable to life. They prevent such awful things as cuts, sores, and suffering. They are wonderful!" "Well, then, why don't you wear them?" I asked, bewildered. "Ah," said he, "that is just it. Why don't we?"

I checked in and went directly to the coffee shop. There I deliberately sat down by a friendly looking man who likewise wore no shoes. When we had finished eating, we walked out of the hotel. He pointed to a huge brick building. "You see that?" he said with pride. "That is one of our outstanding shoe manufacturing establishments." "You mean you make shoes there?" I asked. "Well, not exactly," he said, a bit ashamed. "We talk about making shoes there and, believe me, we've got one of the best and most brilliant speakers you have ever heard. He talks every week on this great subject of shoes. Just yesterday he moved the people profoundly on the necessity of shoe-wearing. It was really wonderful!" "But why don't you wear them?" I said, insistently. "Ah," he said, "that is just it. Why don't we?"

I could take it no longer. I left my friend and went to my room. There, sitting in *The City of*

Everywhere, a question rang in my ears: Why don't we? *Why don't we?* WHY DON'T WE?...³

In spite of the Negro spiritual that says "all God's chilluns got shoes," it would appear that not everyone is wearing them. Not all wear the gospel shoes to protect from corruption and injury; not all are shod with the army boots of gospel warfare.

When God asked Moses to confront Pharaoh and liberate Israel, Moses made the excuse, "I cannot speak." Gideon begged off with, "My family is poor—and I am least in my father's house." Saul, about to be made king, hid himself among the baggage (1 Samuel 10:22). Characters in Jesus' story of the king's wedding feast excused themselves with, "I've just bought a yoke of oxen," and "I married a wife."

What's our excuse?

If we are to discharge our obligation to the kingdom of God, we must retreat to the abundance of God's providence and grace. By His grace, we are able—able to uproot mulberry trees and to throw mountains into the sea.

Why not respond to our commission as expressed in Henry Frost's poem?

COMMISSIONED

Out from the realm of the glory light
Into the far-away land of night,
Out from the bliss of worshipful song
Into the pain of hatred and wrong,
Out from the holy rapture above
Into the grief of rejected love,

Out from the life at the Father's side
Into the death of the crucified,
Out of high honor and into shame
The Master, willingly, gladly came:

And now, since He may not suffer anew,
As the Father sent Him, so sendeth He
you![4]

Chapter 8, Notes

1.   See F. F. Bruce, *Tyndale New Testament Commentary: Romans* (revised) (Wheaton, Ill: Tyndale, 1985), p. 147.

2.   Tim Hansel, *You Gotta Keep Dancin'* (Elgin, Ill.: David C. Cook, 1985), p. 87.

3.   Adapted from Hugh Price Hughes, *City of Everywhere*, cited by Rev. Howard Stone Anderson, D. D., *Chaplain*, July 1947.

4.   Henry Frost, "Commissioned," *Doorstep Evangel*, vol. 1, no. 10.

CHAPTER 9

The Return
of the Ark

"**F**RIDAY'S here, but Sunday's comin'!"

Tony Campolo's dramatic sermon by that name lifts the hearer from the hopelessness of the crucifixion to the triumph of the resurrection, from "we had hoped" to "He is risen!" The sermon virtually sings!

By repetition, increased tempo, and exultant proclamation, triumph bursts from the tragedy of the tomb. The crescendo of the message's refrain carries the listener not only back to Christ's triumph but also assures him that his own tragedies may turn to triumphs in Christ.

Yes! Gloriously yes, Friday's here, but Sunday's comin'!

The same words could be used to declare the triumph of the journeys of the ark of God—the ark which God delivered into captivity, into the hands of the enemy (Psalm 78:61). The God of the ark defeated the enemy and brought the ark back to His people, ultimately to the city of David.

Yes, Sunday is coming. The kingdom is coming. Just as the ark was carried from Philistia to Beth

Shemesh, to Kiriath Jearim, to the house of Obed-Edom, and eventually under King David to Jerusalem, so God in Christ will come to Jerusalem to establish His personal, glorious reign over the whole world.

With that in view, let's follow the ark's journey and ponder what it can mean to us.

The Journey of the Ark

Seven long months of the ark's captivity in Philistia left Israel in doubt and despair. An empty tabernacle. No display of miraculous power. Neither cloud by day nor pillar of fire by night. God had withdrawn His glorious, visible presence.

And yet, as Paul said, "he left not himself without witness," (Acts 14:17, KJV) and "he is not far from each one of us" (Acts 17:27). Though not gloriously, *visibly* present, yet God was at work as a sort of undercover agent.

While captive, the ark-dwelling presence of God was neither helpless nor idle. The Lord broke in pieces the idol Dagon, and in succession plagued the cities of Ashdod, Gath, and Ekron. The Philistines sent the captive ark from city to city to escape the heavy hand of the divine presence in it. In their desperation, the Ekronites called for the leaders of Philistia to send the ark back to Israel. Thus both the government and the religion of Philistia acknowledged and came to fear the God of Israel.

The Philistines placed the ark upon an oxcart and hitched two unbroken cows to it, each with a nursing calf. The calves were kept at home, separated from their mothers. The priests and diviners reasoned that if the ark reached Israel under these conditions, it could not be a matter of chance. That had to mean the hand of God was in it. And so it came to pass.

The "captive" God was in control after all.

The Long Road Home

The ark took a long time in getting home. As we trace its journeys from Ekron in Philistia to Beth

Shemesh in Israel, from there to Kiriath Jearim, where it remained for twenty years, and from Kiriath Jearim to Jerusalem, we see an interplay between God's sovereignty and man's free will.

In Philistia the ark was carried from city to city because the hand of the Lord was heavy upon the nation (1 Samuel 5:6-12).

At Beth Shemesh the people celebrated the return of the ark with burnt offerings and sacrifices, but their joy turned to sorrow when God struck down a great number of men who presumed to look into the ark. As a result, they asked the people of Kiriath Jearim to take the ark away (1 Samuel 6:19-20, KJV).

God's heavy and holy hand first prompted Israel's enemy, and then a city in Israel, to ask that His presence in judgment be removed from them (1 Samuel 5:11, 6:20-21).

The move toward Jerusalem and the heart of Israel was prompted by David's love for the Lord. "All Israel" joined David and the priests and Levites to celebrate as the ark was brought toward the holy city. But disaster struck. Somehow no one thought to carry the ark upon shoulders of two priests as God had instructed Moses. Instead an oxcart was used, accompanied by Uzzah and Ahio.

The oxen stumbled as they pulled the cart, and Uzzah put his hand on the ark to steady it. Immediately God struck him dead. David responded in anger and fear, and the ark was taken to the house of Obed-Edom, where it stayed for three months (1 Chronicles 13:11-13), "and the LORD blessed his household and everything he had" (1 Chronicles 13:14).

A second time David sought to bring the ark of God to Jerusalem and to the tent he had pitched for it (1 Chronicles 15:1). This time the king remembered that "no one but the Levites may carry the ark of God" (1 Chronicles 15:2). So again David gathered all Israel to bring up the ark, with singing, "with shouts, with the sounding of rams' horns and trumpets, and of cymbals, and the playing of lyres and harps" (1 Chronicles 15:28).

The Duties of Ark Bearers

David's understanding that no one but the Levites could carry the ark of God may well have come through the words of Numbers, chapters three and four. In these chapters God instructs the Levites concerning their duties in connection with the tabernacle, and particularly those duties relating to the transportation of its parts and sacred furniture. The sons of Gershon (Numbers 3:25-26) and the sons of Merari (Numbers 3:36) were to take down, transport, and erect the heavier parts of the tabernacle and were given oxen and oxcarts to help in the task (Numbers 7:1-8). "But Moses did not give any to the Kohathites, because they were to carry on their shoulders the holy things, for which they were responsible" (Numbers 7:9).

The burdens which the Kohathites carried were the "most holy things" (Numbers 4:4-19). These included the ark of the testimony, the table of shewbread, the golden lampstand, the golden altar, the brazen altar, and the utensils of service.

The specific burden of a Kohathite was divinely appointed through Aaron and his sons (Numbers 4:19).

The Kohathites bore the very presence of God in the ark of the LORD (Numbers 4:5). They were not allowed to touch or to see the holy things they carried (Numbers 4:15, 20).

The Significance of Ark Bearers

You may be wondering why I have presented in some detail the priestly duties connected with the tabernacle and the ark. There are several reasons.

1. The duties graphically portray the spiritual responsibilities of believer-priests today.

As believer-priests after the example of the Kohathites, we must bear upon our own shoulders the burden of the "most holy things." As the apostle Paul put it, "while we are in this tent, we groan and are burdened" (2 Corinthians 5:4).

There are some burdens, such as the cares of this life, which we should discard and put upon the Lord. In the words of the apostle Peter, we are to humble ourselves under the mighty hand of God and to "cast all your anxiety on him because he cares for you" (1 Peter 5:7).

But there are some burdens which God has appointed for us. Galatians 6:5 points out that burden-bearing is the common lot of mankind by saying that "each one should carry his own load."

The Kohathites served God in the tabernacle designed by God to be His dwelling place in the midst of His people. Believers today carry the burdens involved in making our bodies fit temples of the Holy Spirit (1 Corinthians 6:19-20). As typified by the burdens of the priestly family, our burdens are appointed by God, they are a service to Him, they must be personally borne upon our own shoulders, and their glory is hidden from our eyes.

2. They explain God's appointed and approved way for moving the ark.

It was the ark of God, the ark of His presence, and yet it had to be carried upon the shoulders of two priests. Certainly God could have used some sort of hovercraft like Ezekiel's wheels to convey His presence from place to place without help from His human children. But He didn't.

Didn't Isaiah ridicule the idols of the heathen nations surrounding Israel because they were a burden to the beasts, to their wagons, and to the shoulders of men? (Isaiah 46:1-2) And was it not a custom for nations to carry away the gods of nations they had conquered? (Jeremiah 48:7)

Why, then, did the true God see fit to dwell in a sanctuary and symbol which had to be borne on the shoulders of men and was allowed to be taken captive, just as the idols of surrounding nations? The answer, at least in part, is that God has limited Himself to human cooperation. Hence our Lord Jesus Christ instructed us to pray, "your kingdom come, your will be done on earth as it is in heaven" (Matthew 6:10).

If the ark on the shoulders of the Kohathites represents human cooperation in carrying out the will of God, the ark on the oxcart portrays God's sovereignty in carrying out His will. And the ark of God carried by wicked men, such as Hophni and Phinehas, deprived Israel of the glory of God and caused defeat in battle. But the ark carried according to God's appointed order and headed toward the heart of the nation, as in David's day, brought joy and gladness.

The carried ark of God's presence teaches us that when God wants to go someplace to bless someone, He is normally dependent upon us to take Him there. Or to put it in the language of the believer's relation to Christ, we are His body, His hands and feet, and what He would do on earth, He does through us (Ephesians 1:23).

The Return to Jerusalem

And now, at last, let us consider the return of the ark to Jerusalem under David as foreshadowing the return of Jesus Christ to establish His kingdom on earth. And I shall ask: Is there something we need to do to hasten that Ultimate Presence of God toward His resting place in the holy city?

First, note that the ark marked the dwelling place and presence of God in the early history of Israel. Correspondingly, the Lord Jesus Christ, in whom dwells all the fullness of the Godhead bodily (Colossians 2:9), replaced the gold-covered wooden box with human flesh to become the ultimate revelation of God. He is God manifest in the flesh (1 Timothy 3:16). And the hope of Israel and of the church will be realized when He comes in glory and power to earth and to Jerusalem.

That hope rose inside the disciples of Jesus following His resurrection. They asked Him, "Lord, are you at this time going to restore the kingdom to Israel?" (Acts 1:6).

The *time* of His return, Jesus told them, was in His Father's hands, but the *fact* of His return was assured by two angels as Jesus ascended into heaven. "Men of Galilee," they said, "why do you stand here looking into the sky? This same Jesus, who has been taken from you into heaven, will come back in the same way you have seen him go into heaven" (Acts 1:11).

In His first coming He was as the ark of God's strength and glory delivered captive into the hands of His enemies. When He comes again, He will come as Lord of lords and King of kings (Revelation 17:14) in power and great glory. He will be the ark triumphant, the ark reigning from Jerusalem.

Jesus as the Ark

The names of the ark found in the Old Testament find their ultimate significance in describing the presence of God when applied to the Lord Jesus Christ.

He is the ark of God. He is the eternal Word who was with God and was God (John 1:1). He is the creator (Colossians 1:16). He became incarnate. "The Word was made flesh, and dwelt among us, (and we beheld his glory, the glory as of the only begotten of the Father), full of grace and truth" (John 1:14, KJV).

Because He and the Father were of one essence, equal in power and glory, Jesus could say, "Anyone who has seen me has seen the Father" (John 14:9).

He is the ark of the LORD. This is the name which proclaims the saving and redemptive work of God, in that LORD was the name by which God revealed Himself to Moses and to the children of Israel when He brought them out of slavery in Egypt (Exodus 3:14,15). LORD became the name of God commonly associated with salvation.

He is also the ark of the Testimony (Exodus 25:22). The ark became the repository of the law of God. And in Jesus Christ the law found perfect expression. He loved God and man supremely. He lived "without spot or blemish" in moral purity. He honored and satisfied the law's demands against guilty sinners by dying in their place. He came not to destroy, but to fulfill the law (Matthew 5:17). He is Jesus Christ the righteous (1 John 2:1), the ark of the Testimony.

Jesus Christ is the ark of God's might (Psalm 78:61). For our salvation God delivered the ark of His might into captivity, and His glory into the enemy's hand. The One who had power to lay down his life and to take it up again (John 10:17-18) was crucified through weakness (2 Corinthians 13:4). The paradox of divine power, as explained to the apostle Paul, was exemplified in the death of Christ: "My power is made perfect in weakness" (2 Corinthians 12:9).

But when He comes again as the ark of God's strength, He will come in power and great glory to right the wrongs of earth and to rule in equity and justice.

With the psalmist we must pray for the ark to come to Zion, His resting place, and to usher in the golden age. Won't you join me in such a prayer?

Arise, O LORD, and come to your resting place,
you and the ark of your might (Psalm 132:8).

The Final Triumph

Jesus is coming to rule over the earth—returning from captivity, breaking jail, as it were, to be invested with throne rights. This time His triumphal entry will not end in the irony and agony of the cross. Never again will His strength and glory be delivered into captivity. No, never!

For "when the Son of Man comes in his glory, and all the angels with him, he will sit on his throne in heavenly glory," (Matthew 25:31) and He will gather everyone before Him and will judge all the nations.

This means there will be a change in government. Satan, who once tempted Jesus to worship him by promising to give all the kingdoms of the world, will be stripped of his authority and cast into the abyss (Revelation 20:3).

God will no longer have to accomplish His purposes under governments which deny His existence and oppose all His plans. Jesus will no longer pay taxes to Caesar. He will rule with a rod of iron (Revelation 12:5). "He will judge the world in righteousness; he will govern the peoples with justice" (Psalm 9:8). And, in turn, the peoples of the world will learn righteousness, as is stated in the words of Isaiah: "When your judgments come upon the earth, the people of the world learn righteousness" (Isaiah 26:9).

This will mean a different and favorable climate in which to make moral decisions. Satan will be bound, and people will not be blinded by his deceptions. It will no longer be the smart and accepted thing to "call evil good and good evil," to "put darkness for light and light for darkness," or to "put bitter for sweet and sweet for bitter" (Isaiah 5:20).

There will be no demands for legal recognition of perverted lifestyles. Mafia chieftains will not buy government protection. Purveyors of pornographic filth will not call for protection under free speech guarantees. The government will not pay for abortions. There will be no need for the American Civil Liberties Union.

In one way or another, idealistic men and women of all the ages have envisioned and tried to bring about a golden age. Our Lord Jesus Christ will usher in such an age when He comes to set up God's kingdom upon earth. The gospel of His saving grace now saves men from their iniquities. The gospel of the kingdom offers salvation from inequities as well.

The meek *shall* inherit the earth.

The beatitudes of our Lord look to His coming kingdom for their full realization. Let us look at them and direct our thinking to the glorious day when they shall describe God's redeemed society:

> Blessed are the poor in spirit,
>> for theirs is the kingdom of heaven.
> Blessed are those who mourn,
>> for they will be comforted.
> Blessed are the meek,
>> for they will inherit the earth.
> Blessed are those who hunger and thirst for righteousness,
>> for they will be filled.
> Blessed are the merciful,
>> for they will be shown mercy.
> Blessed are the pure in heart,
>> for they will see God.
> Blessed are the peacemakers,
>> for they will be called sons of God.
> Blessed are those who are persecuted
>> because of righteousness,
>> for theirs is the kingdom of heaven
>>> (Matthew 5:3-10).

Perhaps James summarized it best when he wrote to his friends, "Hath not God chosen the poor of this world rich in faith, and heirs of the kingdom which he hath promised to them that love him?" (James 2:5, KJV).

Poverty per se does not guarantee a place in the coming kingdom, but a lack of material things leading to poverty of spirit and humility before God promises the kingdom of heaven. To those who are not proud and self-supporting spiritually—to the poor in spirit—God gives grace and the kingdom (James 4:6). Not to the proud and the powerful, but to the meek.

Can we hasten the day of Christ's return and the establishment of His kingdom? We can pray, even as He instructed us:

> Our Father in heaven,
> hallowed be your name,
> your kingdom come,
> your will be done
>   on earth as it is in heaven (Matthew 6:9-10).

Even so, come Lord Jesus!

CHAPTER 10

If You Had Been Here— A Second Opinion

HAS God indeed been taken captive? Has omnipotence really been bound? Must we despair of having His personal presence and help in time of temptation and trial?

I want a second opinion!

Second opinions can be lifesavers . . . and money-savers. Once I saved nearly three hundred dollars by following the suggestion of my new insurance company that I secure a second opinion about some dental work.

A second opinion about the subject matter of the preceding chapters does not mean we have turned to a different Carrier for our assurance of help in trials and hope of eternal life. Nor does it mean that the Bible says both yes and no.

It simply means that God's truth, like a skillfully cut diamond, has many facets, and we wish to catch the sparkle of another side of it.

To say with the psalmist that God "delivered his strength into captivity and his glory into the enemy's hand" is to affirm that God imposed certain limitations upon Himself.

And if indeed this sheds light upon His providential dealings with the world and His own within the world, it will help us to understand the boundary conditions under which we may expect to receive help from Him.

Bear in mind that captivity does not mean helplessness. Omnipotence has not become impotence. The absence of His glorious, sovereign, manifest presence does not mean He is not really and powerfully present and working. Unlike Adoni-Bezek, God's thumbs and big toes have not been cut off. He can still stand and wield His mighty sword. And in His wise providence it is often the "sword of the LORD, and of Gideon" (Judges 7:18, KJV).

The Presence of God in His Absence

When I affirm the absence of God's glorious, overwhelming, visible presence—a planned limitation of His power—and yet assert that He is present as an available, powerful, unseen helper, I am not engaging in the sort of fancy expressed in these verses:

> As I was coming up the stair,
> I met a man who wasn't there.
> He wasn't there again today;
> I wish that man would go away.

On the contrary, what I am saying is illustrated in three of our best-loved Psalms.

Psalms 22 and 23 have to do with the perception of God's unseen presence, and Psalm 24 anticipates the sight of His glorious, visible presence reigning in power and majesty in the holy city.

In Psalm 22 the psalmist (and the Messiah) first despairs of God's presence and then declares it. First the cry of desolation, then the affirmation of faith—a sequence familiar in the Psalms.

The psalmist's despair, and our own, found its ultimate expression in Jesus' cry of desolation when He died for our sins upon the cross. Because He was "made sin for us" and bore the wrath of God as our substitute, He cried out, "My God, my God, why have you forsaken me? Why are you so far from saving me, so far from the words of my groaning?" (v. 1).

Psalm 69:20 added new dimension to my understanding of the sufferings of Christ on our behalf: "Reproach has broken my heart, and I am so sick" (NASB).

Later in Psalm 22, triumphant faith responds, "You have answered Me. . . . You who fear the LORD, praise Him! . . . For He has not despised nor abhorred the affliction of the afflicted; Nor has He hidden His face from Him; But when He cried to Him, He heard" (vv. 21, 23-24, NKJV).

In Psalm 23 the invisible, powerful, and caring presence of God becomes the Good Shepherd to the eye of faith, enabling the believer to say, "The LORD is my shepherd, I shall not be in want. . . . Even though I walk through the valley of the shadow of death, I will fear no evil, for you are with me; your rod and your staff, they comfort me."

He Is Coming in Glory

As we saw in the previous chapter, God will one day send His Son to establish a glorious, visible presence and reign on the earth. To that end the holy city is asked to open its gates to Him who has the right to rule:

Lift up your heads, O you gates;
 be lifted up, you ancient doors,
 that the King of glory may come in.
Who is this King of glory?
 The LORD strong and mighty,
 the LORD mighty in battle (Psalm 24:7, 8).

But until the day of His glorious appearing, our experience often parallels that of Mary and Martha when their brother Lazarus became sick. They sent for Jesus to come, believing that He could heal their brother. But Jesus did not come until Lazarus had died and was in the grave four days. Each sister voiced the same faith and the same word of reproach: "Lord, if you had been here, my brother would not have died" (John 11:21, 32).

Jesus delayed in coming not because He was indifferent, but because He was about to do something for the glory of God. The biblical account tells us that "Jesus loved Martha and her sister and Lazarus" (John 11:5) and that when He heard that Lazarus was sick, "he stayed where he was two more days" (11:6).

Who would not share Mary and Martha's feeling that if Jesus really loved them, He would respond immediately to their need? But no, He delayed His coming until Lazarus was dead. He permitted their sorrow, left their prayers seemingly unanswered. He had a better plan—for the glory of God. He raised Lazarus from the dead, and proved that He was indeed the resurrection and the life. His was "tough love."

Is He a God Who "Can't Be Bothered"?

Sometimes we question God's friendship because it seems He "can't be bothered" with our needs, even when we come into His presence in desperate prayer.

What could be worse than to believe that God can't be bothered with our needs? The Old Testament prophet Elijah taunted the prophets of Baal with something like that. Do you recall the story?

It was a showdown between the LORD and Baal, prompted by Israel's departure from the worship of the true God under the influence of wicked King Ahab and his wife Jezebel. Elijah wanted to persuade his countrymen to return to worship the LORD alone. Two altars and two sacrifices were prepared—one for the worship of

Baal and one for the LORD. Then Elijah laid down the rules of the contest: "You call on the name of your god, and I will call on the name of the LORD. The god who answers by fire—he is God" (1 Kings 18:24).

The prophets of Baal pled in vain for Baal to send fire to ignite the wood under their sacrifice. They cut themselves, they prophesied, and they cried out, "O Baal, answer us!" But the skies were silent.

Elijah took the opportunity to taunt them: "Shout louder! Surely he is a god! Perhaps he is deep in thought, or busy, or traveling. Maybe he is sleeping and must be awakened" (1 Kings 18:27).

The prophets shouted louder and slashed themselves with swords and cried out all afternoon until evening. "But there was no response, no one answered, no one paid attention" (1 Kings 18:29).

Now, it is fine that there was no response, no answer, no fire from Baal; he is not God. But when we go to the Lord God Almighty at the midnight hour of our desperate need, we need an answer—and it must not be, "Don't bother me."

In Mary and Martha's case, we have the advantage of knowing the end of the story. The Lord delayed so that He might raise Lazarus from the dead to the glory of God. But Mary and Martha did not know this. Certainly Jesus was not present at the death of Lazarus. He did not keep Lazarus from dying; neither did He spare Martha and Mary the sorrows of bereavement or from doubts concerning His love. Nevertheless, He knew the hour of Lazarus's death and later wept at his tomb.

In view of His own death, resurrection, and ascension to the Father, Jesus spoke of the coming of the Holy Spirit to be an indwelling Comforter in the heart of every believer. He said to His disciples, "I will pray the Father, and he shall give you another Comforter, that he may abide with you for ever" (John 14:16, KJV).

It was in light of the promised Comforter or Helper that Jesus said, "It is expedient for you that I go away: for if I go not away, the Comforter will not come unto you; but if I depart, I will send him unto you" (John 16:7, KJV).

The Comforter Provides a New Intimacy with God

The coming of the Holy Spirit on the day of Pentecost to form the body of Christ and to indwell individual believing hearts marks a new level of intimacy with God's presence and a new availability of His power. Jesus said concerning the ministry of the Holy Spirit, "He lives with you and will be in you" (John 14:17).

In times of disappointment, defeat, and despair, we may doubt the presence and care of God. It is just then that we need to remind ourselves of His promises to be with us. Let us hide in our hearts such promises as the following:

God said to Moses, "My Presence will go with you" (Exodus 33:14).

God promised Joshua, "I will be with you; I will never leave you nor forsake you" (Joshua 1:5).

That same promise is repeated to believers today: "Never will I leave you; never will I forsake you" (Hebrews 13:5). To this add the words of Jesus: "I will not leave you as orphans; I will come to you" (John 14:18). And "All authority in heaven and on earth has been given to me. . . . And surely I am with you always, to the very end of the age" (Matthew 28:18, 20).

But we are inclined to skepticism and to say with Gideon, "If the LORD is with us, why has all this happened to us?" (Judges 6:13).

Enjoyment of God's presence in the believer's heart is based upon faith and obedience. We do not experience instant and automatic victory over sin and relief from trials and suffering simply because of His indwelling presence.

Remember that in the days of Samuel, the ark of God's presence was taken captive by the Philistines and the armies of Israel suffered defeat because of Israel's sin. Later on, the mishandled ark brought death to Uzzah.

And since during this age believers form the temple of God, defiling the temple brings judgment, while cleansing our heart-temples brings the realization of God's indwelling presence and benevolent Fatherhood (1 Corinthians 3:17, 2 Corinthians 6:16-18).

We Serve as Priests in Our Heart-Temples

As believer-priests we serve God in our own heart-temples. Just as the priests in Israel were required to arise before sunrise and to cleanse the temple by picking up the litter and refuse from the previous day's worship, so the believer-priest needs to cleanse his heart daily by confession of sin and by committing his life to the Lord.

The ancient priests in Israel cleaned up the temple before dawn and by torchlight.[1] The believer-priest today is to search his heart at the beginning of the day by the light of the word of God. Failure to cleanse our hearts before God may forfeit the realized blessing of God's presence. The following anonymous poem expresses it well:

THE SECRET

I met God in the morning,
When my day was at its best
And His presence came like sunrise,
Like a glory in my breast.
All day long the Presence lingered;
All day long He stayed with me;
And we sailed in perfect calmness
O'er a very troubled sea.
Other ships were blown and battered,
Other ships were sore distressed,
But the winds that seemed to drive them

Brought to us a peace and rest.
Then I thought of other mornings,
With a keen remorse of mind.
When I too had loosed the moorings
With the Presence left behind.
So, I think I know the secret,
Learned from many a troubled way;
You must seek Him in the morning
If you want Him through the day.[2]

Our experience could be like that of the psalmist who often complained that God hid His face: "Why, O LORD, do you stand far off? Why do you hide yourself in times of trouble?" (Psalm 10:1).

Jesus likened His relationship to His disciples to the union between a grapevine and its branches. He said, "I am the vine, ye are the branches; He that abideth in me, and I in him, the same bringeth forth much fruit: for without me ye can do nothing" (John 15:5, KJV).

If we are to be fruitful believers, consciously drawing life and fruit from His presence, we must abide in Him, have our life in Him. For without Him, we can do nothing.

We Must Rely on His Presence

We are constantly to be filled with the Spirit and to walk in dependence upon Him: "Do not get drunk on wine, which leads to debauchery. Instead, be filled with the Spirit," and again, "Live by the Spirit, and you will not gratify the desires of the sinful nature" (Ephesians 5:18, Galatians 5:16).

To benefit from the fact of God's indwelling presence in our struggles and sufferings, we must live in awareness of His presence and be in right relation to it. We must learn to practice His presence and to count upon it.

It was by counting upon the presence and power of the indwelling Christ that Joe Maddock, my high school Sunday school teacher, kicked the cigarette habit.

Again and again he tried to quit, only to sneak back to the pack. Finally, in utter desperation, he got down on his knees before God and took a step of bold faith based upon his belief that Christ actually lived in his heart. First he quoted Galatians 2:20: "I have been crucified with Christ and I no longer live, but Christ lives in me." Then, appropriating by faith the fact of Christ's indwelling presence, he cried out, "Christ, if you want to smoke, go ahead."

Christ did not want to smoke and the habit was broken.

That is always the way to freedom in Christ: First acknowledge His presence and power, then act upon that knowledge.

You can do that right now. No matter the trials you face, no matter the obstacles or personal history or anguish or temptations that you face, you *can* live to the glory of God even in the middle of difficult circumstances. Starting this instant. I don't mean that your problems will dissolve or limp meekly away; I *do* mean you can live as a testimony to God's power even in the midst of them.

What Can I Expect?

If God is indeed an indwelling and enabling presence in the heart of every believer, are His presence and power limited because He "delivered his strength into captivity, and his glory into the enemy's hand"?

On the contrary, understanding God's self-imposed limitations may aid us in two ways: It will enable us to get help from God's indwelling presence; and it will increase our awareness that God needs our help to accomplish His moral and redemptive purposes. When God casts the devil and his angels out of heaven, He will use Michael and his angels to do it. And in bringing salvation to a lost world, He counts upon the prayers and service of the church.

The Captivity of God—A Review

The capture of the ark of God by the Philistines begins the story of God's activity as a captive under an alien government and a false religion. He did not overthrow the government, nor put an end to the worship of Dagon.

But His presence in the captured ark visited city after city with a dreadful plague so that the Philistines were made to acknowledge and to "give glory to the God of Israel" (1 Samuel 6:5, NKJV).

Let's suppose that the warriors of Philistia captured a number of Israelite soldiers and forced them to carry the ark into the temple of Dagon. No doubt it would have been a comfort to them to have known God's game plan.

It surely would have helped Peter. You remember Peter—the one-man army whose sword cut off the ear of the high priest's servant. Yet because he didn't understand, he denied his captured Lord on His way to the cross.

Like Peter who followed his captive Lord—unfortunately, "afar off"—and like Simon the Cyrenian who was forced to bear His cross, so God's people follow a God who sent His power and glory into captivity and allows His people to enter into His humiliation . . . and glory! (see John 13:31, Romans 8:17, Philippians 2:5-11)

To this day God and His redeemed people live, and suffer, in a world dominated by Satan, under governments which often persecute the godly. But while we believe God is in ultimate control, that "ultimate" seems so far away . . . especially when we need Him *near*. In the meantime, God is working under the circumstances.

These "circumstances" form the boundary conditions, or limitations, under which His presence and power are manifested.

Millions of people have been enslaved within barbed wire boundaries. Uncounted others have been kept in the dismal holding pens of disease, suffering, and despair. Still others are regimented behind the Berlin walls of the drabness of the ordinary. And their release calls for more than merchandiser Norm Thompson's "escape from the ordinary."

But the lines for many have fallen in pleasant places. Rail fences painted white mark out their pleasant estates.

The apostle Paul told the philosophers of Athens that God had determined the times and boundaries of the nations so that they should seek the Lord (Acts 17:26-27).

The barbed wire boundaries have yielded a harvest of souls whose afflictions caused them to turn to God. And some of the people of the white-fenced estates, knowing something of the "all things" God has given us "richly to enjoy," have learned that the goodness of God leads to repentance.

How, then, can we—how can I—enjoy the fullness of God's indwelling presence? What can I expect by way of answered prayer?

Well, what are the boundary conditions? God's basic boundaries are set to help us seek Him, to be conformed to Christ. And Christ challenges us to a life of self-denial and cross-bearing (Luke 9:23). The apostle Paul wanted to know Christ and the power of His resurrection and the fellowship of His sufferings, being conformed to His death (Philippians 3:10). The apostle Peter wrote of the testing of our faith and of fiery trials as things to be expected—not much said of pleasure as an end in itself.

Are we more concerned about escape from our boundary conditions—or enjoying them—than we are committed to know God's purpose in and through them?

God is not so much concerned about getting us out of trials as in causing us to grow through them. And He manifests His presence and power in them.

So it was with Bill Talbott, my wife's brother-in-law. He was suffering pain so excruciating that he would bang his head on the floor as diversionary relief. But in his pain Christ became so real to him that he expressed his willingness to endure the pain provided Christ would again manifest Himself.

I cannot speak to you from personal experience about God's comforting and sustaining presence in all the boundary conditions of life, because I have not experienced much of them. Others have known it and give faithful testimony of it.

But as for me, "The lines have fallen unto me in pleasant places; yea, I have a goodly heritage" (Psalm 16:6, KJV). My boundary lines have been akin to the white-painted fences.

I was born into a Christian home. Dad and mother loved the Lord and all six of their children came to know Him. I graduated from Wheaton College and Dallas Seminary, and under the leadership of John G. Mitchell I became a co-founder of Multnomah School of the Bible. In the course of time I married Doris Coffin, Multnomah's dean of women. To us were born five girls and four boys, all of whom love and serve the Lord.

As the family grew in number we moved to an eight-acre farm. Our principal crop was children. And the farm was an idyllic place to rear them:

> an orchard of apples and prunes,
> a dairy farm,
> an alfalfa field,
> an acre-and-a-half pond,
> a large garden.

Our farm population included horses, cows, calves, chickens, ducks, rabbits, and, on occasion, a pig or two.

While the little farm was not actually enclosed by a white-picket fence, it provided those providential boundary conditions of health and happiness which caused us to rejoice in the goodness of God.

There were answers to prayer:

- A five-hundred-dollar gift from a friend became the down payment enabling us to buy the farm;

- A five-thousand-dollar gift from an unknown friend covered the cost of enlarging the house to encompass our large family.

But into the pleasant lines which had fallen to us intruded sickness and death. Jane, our oldest child, was stricken in junior high school with polio. It was for her an encounter with God as well as with polio, and like Jacob of old, she has ever since walked with a limp.

And Doris, beloved wife and needed mother of nine small children, died as a result of an automobile accident. Her death was an answer to prayer we did not expect or want. For the twenty-two days she lay unconscious in the hospital, hundreds—if not thousands—of her friends prayed for her recovery. But she went into the Lord's presence without regaining consciousness and apparently without suffering. She experienced that "ultimate healing" which comes from being in the Lord's presence (2 Corinthians 5:1-8). For this assurance her family rejoiced then and does so now.

But we had been bereaved. What Job said about his experience we could say about ours: "When I looked for good, then evil came unto me" (Job 30:26, KJV).

As a family we felt on firm ground in expecting God to heal her. I needed her love, her spiritual insight, and her encouragement. Her children needed her. Her homey column, "Out of the Mixing Bowl," was read by thousands. At the time of her accident she was on her way to Springfield, Oregon, to speak at a women's luncheon, a frequent ministry.

At the time death entered the theretofore pleasant boundaries of our life, it had never entered my mind that God had sent His glory and strength into captivity and that I could draw comfort, strength, and even challenge from such an amazing self-limitation. But I can see now that some of the truths have direct and helpful application.

First, God is bound by His love. What He allowed, He did so in His love.

Second, God is captive to a moral plan. He causes the rain to fall upon the just and the unjust. And "accidents happen" to His loved ones as well as to those far from Him.

Third, His beloved people become casualties as did His Son. And His greatest victories are often seen in the casualties who die trusting Him. It may be that those we see as casualties actually may be victors called home to reward.

Fourth, the "over/under principle" outlined in the epilogue—that the sovereign God, in ultimate control "over" all, often works best "under" the circumstances—was truly evident in Doris's death. We firmly believe (and with comfort!) that for reasons unknown to us, God wanted Doris in heaven and that in His appointed time the circumstances occurred which took her life.

So shall it always be until the time when the kingdoms of this earth shall become the kingdom of our Lord and Savior. Until then, His people may experience suffering by "chance" or at the hands of the rulers of this age—but also great deliverances and great experiences of His presence.

Whatever the providential boundaries in which you find yourself, God wants to come into your life to enrich it and to prepare you for His approving presence—both in time and for eternity.

Our Lord Jesus Christ spoke of this great desire of God in Revelation 3:20:

> Behold, I stand at the door and knock. If anyone hears My voice and opens the door, I will come in to him and dine with him, and he with Me (NKJV).

I invite you to take Him up on His offer. A better invitation you will never receive.

Chapter 10, Notes

1. Alfred Edersheim, *The Life and Times of Jesus the Messiah,* vol.1 (New York: Longmans, Green, and Co., n.d.), p. 134.

2. "The Secret," *Doorstep Evangel,* vol. 29, no. 12 (July 1967).

Philistines on the Hill of God

THE dual roles of sovereignty and subjection—of control and captivity—can be traced through much of God's dealings with Israel and the surrounding nations.

But before we do that, allow me to tell a story.

Along with several other members of the faculty at Multnomah School of the Bible, I was scheduled to speak at a men's conference. The theme to bind the conference together was "the richness and fullness of the Christian life—above and beyond the ordinary."

My topic, "The Captivity of God—A Key to the Interpretation of History," was hard to fit into this superlative category, so it was listed as "Above the World System."

I said at the lecture that my topic would be better expressed as "Above the World System, Under the World System." It would portray a sovereign God subjecting Himself to authorities He had established. Could we call it the over/under principle?

The over/under principle can be seen in the life of a college president who also teaches. As president he is above the dean of faculty; as teacher he is under him. While it would be hard for the dean to terminate the president's teaching role, the president certainly could relieve the dean of his position and authority.

With that story in mind, let us get on with historical accounts of God's sovereign control *over* the world system, while yet captive *under* the world system.

The God of Slaves in Egypt

In Egypt, the Lord became the God of a slave nation and did not show Himself as the God above all gods until He humbled Egypt with plagues and delivered His people from bondage.

God had promised to give the land of Canaan to Abraham, but his descendants could not take possession for four hundred years. Why not? There were two reasons:

First, the cup of iniquity of the inhabitants of the land was not yet "full." The people were not yet ripe for destruction.

Second, at the time God made the promise to Abraham, this father of an innumerable seed did not have a son. It took time for Abraham's family to develop into a nation capable of carrying on wars of annihilation.

God purposed that Abraham's descendants should dwell in Egypt while they grew into a nation. So He providentially arranged it.

Abraham's grandson, Jacob, with a household of seventy, moved to Egypt during a famine. God had prepared the way for their coming by allowing Jacob's favorite son, Joseph, to be sold into slavery by his jealous brothers. He rose from slavery to become a sovereign second only to Pharaoh, even though he suffered unjust imprisonment along the way.

Did Saved Surpluses Lead to Saving Souls?

God revealed to Pharaoh in a dream that seven years of plenty followed by seven years of famine were coming upon Egypt. Joseph interpreted the dream, and Pharaoh made him responsible for saving the surpluses of the seven good years to care for the lean ones to come.

Because the "God of Abraham, Isaac and Jacob" identified with the Jews as their God, He became the God of a slave people. Both He and His people were under the dominion of Pharaoh and the gods of Egypt until the time He plagued Egypt and her gods and freed His people. It was then that Pharaoh learned the answer to his arrogant question, "Who is the LORD, that I should obey him and let Israel go?" (Exodus 5:2).

And could it have been that the God who sent the famine and caused Egypt to save the surpluses revealed Himself as a Savior of souls? Was it not God's purpose that in Abraham's seed all the nations of the earth were to be blessed? The Egyptians said to Joseph, "Thou hast saved our lives," (Genesis 47:25, KJV). Did this lead them to believe that Joseph's God could save their souls?

In those years when the children of Israel enjoyed favored status as the relatives of Joseph, they "were fruitful, and increased abundantly, and multiplied, and waxed exceeding mighty; and the land was filled with them" (Exodus 1:7, KJV).

But in the course of time a king arose "who knew not Joseph." He feared the numbers and growing power of the Israelites, and so he made slaves of them.

God used Moses to liberate and lead Israel. In calling Moses to the task, God revealed Himself as the God of Abraham, Isaac, and Jacob. He was bound by covenant promises to give their descendants the land of Canaan. When Moses inquired further about His identity, God responded, "This is what you are to say to the Israelites: 'I AM has sent me to you' " (Exodus 3:14). He said in effect, "The God of your fathers is self-existent, independent, sovereign."

God Saw and Cared about Israel's Affliction

The silence of God during Israel's slavery under Egyptian taskmasters did not mean He did not care. He said to Moses, "I have indeed seen the misery of my people in Egypt. . . . I am concerned about their suffering" (Exodus 3:7). So when Moses and his brother Aaron told their enslaved brethren that God had looked on their affliction and was about to deliver them, "they bowed down and worshiped" (Exodus 4:31).

Prior to his commission to deliver the people, Moses, by faith, chose to suffer affliction with his people rather than to enjoy the prestige and pleasure of being called the son of Pharaoh's daughter. "He persevered because he saw him who is invisible" (Hebrews 11:27). And may we, like Moses, when going through trials and temptations with no palpable evidence of God's working, endure as seeing Him who is invisible.

Moreover, the promise of deliverance out of bondage into the Promised Land may have served to comfort the Israelites, especially as they realized that their four hundred years in Egypt were drawing to a close.

God's purpose in redeeming Israel out of slavery in Egypt fits into His plan that all the nations of the world would be blessed in Israel. Through the plagues and the Exodus, Egypt and the surrounding nations came to know that the LORD was God (Exodus 7:5). He broke the silence of four hundred years and spoke deliverance to His people and to all who would receive it—as did the prostitute Rahab.

Judgment and Deliverance in the Time of the Judges

During the time of the judges, which ran from the death of Joshua until the time Saul became king, Israel repeatedly did evil in the sight the LORD, and the LORD delivered one or more tribes into the hands of foreign oppressors. The Israelites suffered terribly and only then cried out to God for relief. God heard their cry and raised up leaders, called judges, to deliver them. Then a period of peace followed which lasted as long as the people served the LORD. Some six times Israel's sin brought judgment, which led to repentance, which brought peace.

The enemies of Israel were religious people who would commonly ascribe their military victories to their gods. The defeat of Israel was considered a defeat of her God. When the enemies of Israel won a military victory and subjugated Israel, they could feel that the God of Israel was defeated. And Israel would have to live under the cloud of worshiping a less-than-omnipotent God.

Was God Defeated When Israel Lost a War?

But there was another way to understand the defeat of Israel: The LORD Himself brought calamity upon His people because they had forsaken Him and worshiped the gods of the nations surrounding them. This certainly represented God as in sovereign control, and many would understand things in this way. But not all, for some continued to believe their victories came because their gods were greater than the LORD. So far as reaching them with the message of salvation was concerned, God would have to break out of captivity to their false belief.

When God raised up judges and led Israel to victory, the nations would have reason to believe that the God of Israel was the true and living God.

Worshiped as One among Many

After Sennacherib, king of Assyria, had conquered and exiled the Northern Kingdom, he settled captives from other nations in Samaria. Because they worshiped the gods of the lands from which they came, God sent lions among them. As a result, they petitioned the king to send them a

Levite to teach them how to worship "the God of the land." As a consequence, "they worshiped the LORD, but they also served their own gods" (2 Kings 17:33).

By allowing Himself to be worshiped along with idols, did God allow Himself to be included in a pantheon? Apparently so, for in spite of prophetic warnings against their idolatrous worship, "even while these people were worshiping the LORD, they were serving their idols" (2 Kings 17:41).

The Over/Under Principle Operating in Babylon

Later, when the people of Judah were carried away captive to Babylon—often called the seat of idolatry—God went with them to be a sanctuary for them (Ezekiel 11:16). There, in the midst of idols, where at times to worship Him was a capital crime, God made princes out of slaves and humbled kings and caused them to testify to the absoluteness of His power and the greatness of His majesty. This provides a beautiful example of the workings of God in captivity—what I have called the over/under principle.

God raised up four young Jewish captives to places of utmost importance and prominence in the government of Babylon during the reigns of several kings. Daniel became an interpreter of dreams and a prized counselor. Like Joseph under Pharaoh, Daniel became second in command under Nebuchadnezzar, and his companions, Shadrach, Meshach, and Abednego, served with him.

These companions showed their faith in the power of God and their indomitable courage in refusing to worship a ninety-foot, golden idol set up by Nebuchadnezzar. They were thrown into a fiery furnace, heated seven times hotter than normal, but came out unscathed, without even the smell of smoke on their garments. This miracle caused Nebuchadnezzar to acknowledge and to praise the God of these three Hebrew young men.

Humbled Emperors Praise Israel's "Captive" God

But later Nebuchadnezzar became filled with pride, and God humbled him by removing him from his throne and giving him the mind and heart of a beast. When the humbling process was complete, God restored the king's mind and returned his throne to him. Then this great king gave testimony to the majesty and power of the Most High "because everything he does is right and all his ways are just" (Daniel 4:37).

Just as God protected Shadrach, Meshach, and Abednego from the fiery furnace, so he kept Daniel from the mouths of the lions. Enemies of Daniel tricked King Darius into making a decree that no prayer should be made to any god or man except the king for thirty days. But Daniel continued to pray three times a day as he knelt before an open window facing Jerusalem. As a result, he was thrown into a den of hungry lions. When Darius found him alive the next morning, he praised and extolled the God of Daniel:

> For he is the living God
> and he endures forever;
> his kingdom will not be destroyed,
> his dominion will never end.
> He rescues and he saves;
> he performs signs and wonders
> in the heavens and on the earth.
> He has rescued Daniel
> from the power of the lions (Daniel 6:26-27).

During the reign of four great emperors, God raised His captive people to places of power and influence, humbled proud kings, and rescued faithful servants. And during this time He unveiled much of the prophetic future through His servant Daniel and the book bearing his name. In addition, God cured His people from idolatry by displaying His power and by exposing the vanity of idols in Babylon.

Sovereign Power Seen in Captivity

Both the sovereign power and the passive captivity of God—the over/under principle—become plain in the looting, defilement, and destruction of the temple by the enemies of Israel.

God exercised and displayed His sovereignty by foretelling the destruction of the temple and by making its desolation a witness against Israel's many sins.

Was God "at home" when such indignities took place, or had He withdrawn? It would appear that at times He was present and at other times He had gone.

Ezekiel described the departure of the glory of the Lord from the temple and from the city as taking place before their destruction by Nebuchadnezzar (Ezekiel 10:18, 11:23). And Jeremiah lamented God's withdrawal of His protecting presence, and cried from a broken heart, "The Lord has rejected his altar and abandoned his sanctuary. He has handed over to the enemy the walls of her palaces" (Lamentations 2:7).

Likewise, the temple could have been desolate and devoid of the presence of God prior to its destruction in A.D. 70. As a part of His lament over the city of Jerusalem, which refused to come to Him, Jesus said, "Look, your house is left to you desolate" (Matthew 23:38).

Temple Raided While God Was at Home

On several occasions, however, the temple was looted or defiled while it still served as the house of God. And to all appearances God was "bound" and did not respond in holy wrath against the intruders. Let us note a few examples.

Shishak, king of Egypt, invaded Judah in the days of king Rehoboam and took away the treasures of the house of the LORD (1 Kings 14:26).

According to the *Biblical Archaeology Review* of May-June 1989, Osorkon I succeeded his father Shishak to the throne and presented "breathtakingly municifent gifts to the gods and goddesses of Egypt." He recorded his gifts on a granite pillar in a temple at Bubastis in the eastern Nile Delta. Fragments of that hieroglyphic text indicate that his gifts totaled at least 383 tons of silver and gold!

Barely five years before Osorkon presented his gifts, his father Shishak had looted the wealth of Jerusalem. Could it be that God allowed Shishak's son to inherit the plundered wealth of Solomon's son Rehoboam and to dedicate it to his gods because Solomon had built temples in Jerusalem to the gods of his foreign wives?

Good king Hezekiah took silver from the house of the LORD and stripped the gold off the temple to give to Sennacherib, king of Assyria, when he invaded the land (2 Kings 18:14-16). God did not rise up to defend His house.

But Sennacherib went too far. He set about to capture the holy city and defied the LORD to defend it. Then it was that God destroyed the army of Sennacherib by a great plague in one night.

Wicked Kings Defile the Temple with Idols

Idolatrous kings erected altars and images of Canaanite gods in the house of God. Manasseh "took the carved Asherah pole he had made and put it in the temple, of which the LORD had said to David and to his son Solomon, 'In this temple and in Jerusalem, which I have chosen out of all the tribes of Israel, I will put my Name forever' " (2 Kings 21:7). Yet there was no bolt of lightening to judge and destroy the one who dared to defile God's house.

The patience of God must have been sorely tried during the time a succession of wicked kings allowed the temple to fall into disrepair and disgrace. It became a place in which to worship Baal, Asherah, and the host of heaven. In time, good king Josiah ordered the temple cleansed and the worship of the LORD restored (2 Kings 23:4).

The second temple, built by the Jewish remnant which Cyrus permitted to return to Jerusalem from their Babylonian captivity, was desecrated by Antiochus Epiphanes in 167 B.C., and in 63 B.C. the Roman general Pompey brazenly entered the holy of holies. Neither was struck dead for his impious act.

Herod's temple replaced the second temple and became the house of God during the days our Lord Jesus lived and taught upon the earth. Because the money changers had made the house of God a den of thieves, Jesus cleansed the temple by driving them out. He also predicted the temple would be destroyed. So it was by Titus in A.D. 70

Did God Change His Place of Earthly Residence?

In the time between the prediction and the fulfillment of the desolation of the temple and the city, it appears God changed His principal place of residence upon the earth. In keeping with Jesus' conversation with the woman at Jacob's well, God's presence was not to be localized and worshiped either on Mount Gerizim or in Jerusalem. Rather, both believing Jew and Gentile were to be "built together to become a dwelling in which God lives by his Spirit" (Ephesians 2:22).

This "holy temple" was formed on the day of Pentecost when the Holy Spirit came to indwell believers and to form the church. It marked a new relation of intimacy between God and His people, from that of being *with* them as in Old Testament days to being a living presence *in* them. John 14:17 records the prophecy and John 17:20-23 the prayer in which Jesus anticipated this new intimacy.

The Story Continued

Just as God allowed His sanctuary to be defiled and destroyed in ancient Israel, so He is permitting the living temple made up of believing human hearts to be subject to destruction. It was incredible to the psalmist Asaph that God did not rouse Himself and rise up and destroy His enemies. His complaint could well be voiced by persecuted Christians today. Let the psalmist's cry be our own:

> Your foes roared in the place where you met with
> us . . .
> They smashed all the carved paneling
>   with their axes and hatchets.
> They burned your sanctuary to the ground;
>   they defiled the dwelling place of your Name.
> They said in their hearts, "We will crush them
> completely!"
>   They burned every place where God was
>   worshiped in the land (Psalm 74:4-8).

Then the psalmist asks God when He is going to stop His enemy from mocking Him, and pleads with God to destroy His enemy:

> How long will the enemy mock you, O God?
>   Will the foe revile your name forever?
> Why do you hold back your hand, your right hand?
> Take it from the folds of your garment and destroy
>   them!
>   (Psalm 74:10-11)

The psalmist's plea, "Rise up, O God, and defend your cause" (Psalm 74:22), has yet to receive its final answer. The enemy continues to mock God, to capture His servants, and to "burn every place where God is worshiped." Instead of being burned, many church buildings today are abandoned and serve instead as museums of art and folklore or are made into restaurants. Something akin to smashing the carved paneling may be seen on the doors of a great cathedral in Beauvais, France. A massive woodcarving of the twelve apostles, mutilated during the French Revolution, displays twelve headless men.

Tradition tells us that the original apostles, except for John, suffered violent deaths.

So it was with John the Baptist, the forerunner of Jesus the Messiah. John was imprisoned by Herod, and in his prison cell began to wonder if Jesus, permitting his imprisonment, was indeed the Messiah.

The Living Temple Suffers Violence

But surely, we may think, has not the resurrection of Jesus Christ and the powerful advent of the Holy Spirit to form and to indwell "the church, which is his body," finished the "captivity" of God and begun a time in which God would powerfully manifest His sovereign majesty?

Not so. The years following Pentecost and the apostolic days until the present time have seen martyrdoms and persecutions unrivaled in history. Some have called these the "silent years." And we walk by faith.

In the providence of God, the sufferings of the body of Christ have a quota not yet filled, and the way to the crown is the way of the cross. In the words of our Lord Jesus Christ, "If anyone would come after me, he must deny himself and take up his cross daily and follow me" (Luke 9:23).

God Manifests His Presence in Enemy Territory

God seems pleased to display His power and wisdom not so much in keeping the faithful from suffering and trials, as in preserving their faith and testimony through them. God is working now, but not as the head of a visible government upon the earth. He does not reign over the earth from a glorious throne. Quite the opposite. The "high place" of His presence and power has often been with His people under an alien government opposed to God.

So it was when Samuel prophesied concerning Saul, whom he had anointed as king of Israel. He predicted that Saul would come to the hill of God and the Spirit of the LORD would come upon him. "You shall come to the hill of God where the Philistine garrison is," Samuel told Saul (1 Samuel 10:5, NKJV).

How often has "the hill of God" been in the hands of an enemy government in occupied territory! Samuel's prophecy described a principle of divine operation. The hill of God was to be found where the garrison of the Philistines was; many years later where the garrison of the Babylonians was; still later where the garrison of the Romans was; and today, Israel's temple site is where the garrison of the Muslims is. (And I might add, that when our hearts become a hill of God, there is a garrison of the Philistines even there.)

Let me repeat: God is not yet ruling over the earth from the promised throne of David. That day is coming, for the day of the LORD will come. Daniel's vision of the stone cut out of a mountain which crushes the colossus of successive human governments declares that God's everlasting kingdom will be established and will rule over the earth.

God Works as an Undercover Agent

But now, today, God most often works as an undercover agent, representing a government in exile. Much of His best work is done where His existence is denied and His rule mocked and despised. He has not shown Himself at His best through temporal power, whether in the church or the state, and least favorably when church and state are combined and claim to represent Him. He has done much of His best work in jail and in the prison camps where His faithful followers suffer for His name.

In the Communist world, where the existence of God is denied and believers are persecuted for their faith, there is mounting evidence that God is present and working in the lives of those who trust Him.

The underground church flourishes with a faith and vitality unmatched in nations where there is freedom to worship—and freedom *not* to worship. From the cata-combs of Rome to the gulags of the Soviet Union, the God who is over all has chosen to be under the world system, underground with His persecuted and precious people . . . suffering with them and sustaining them . . . captive with them.

This is so obviously true that Dr. Don Smith, profes-sor of missions at Western Conservative Baptist Seminary in Portland, Oregon, has remarked that if God wants to do a great work in a nation, He allows it to suffer the deprivations of atheistic Communist rule.

In this epilogue I have presented a principle of God's providential workings called the over/under prin-ciple. God's power and glory came *under* Philistine dominion. But the Scripture tells us that God was in con-trol *over* the situation.

Then I presented instances from the history of God's dealings with Israel and the surrounding nations in which God was manifestly sovereign *over* the circum-stances. And then I reviewed historical events involving God in which He and His people were *under* the circum-stances, the "under the weather" kind—circumstances in which God operated under authorities—both angelic and human—which He had ordained.

When God sent the ark of His might into captivity, His splendor into the hands of the enemy, His visible power and glory went down and disappeared like the set-ting sun.

But the afterglow continues to make radiant the faces of those who trust Him. Beholding the afterglow of the Lord, we are changed. Seeing Him who is invisible, we endure. Understanding in part His captivity, we await the day when Dagon will be destroyed and the ark of His presence returned to Jerusalem.